WHAT DO YOU MEAN —
CHRISTIAN EDUCATION?

What Do You Mean — Christian Education?

Fred Hughes

CARLISLE
THE PATERNOSTER PRESS

British Cataloguing in Publication Data

Hughes, Fred
 What do you mean, Christian education?
 I. Title
 207.41

 ISBN 0 85364 506 X

Typeset by Photoprint, Torquay, Devon
and printed and bound in Great Britain for The Paternoster Press,
P.O. Box 300, Carlisle, CA3 0QS
by The Guernsey Press Co. Ltd., Guernsey, Channel Islands.

Acknowledgements

I am grateful to many people who have contributed in various ways to the writing and publication of this book. Particular credit must go to Viv, my wife, who encouraged me to continue writing, when my inclination was to abandon the task. These chapters were originally a PhD thesis and I want to acknowledge the help of my supervisors at Nottingham University — The Rev Professor John Heywood Thomas and Dr Brian Tolley. I am grateful to the Whitefield Institute, Oxford which paid the university fees, and to its Chairman Dr Oliver Barclay and its Director Dr David Cook who gave valuable encouragement.

I am also grateful to Miss Anthea Cousins and Mrs Winifred Johnson who read the proofs and Mrs Patricia Downes who re-typed Appendix 2. Lastly my thanks to Peter Cousins of Paternoster Press for his interest in getting the manuscript published.

I have endeavoured always to be fair and accurate but I apologise for errors that remain. I trust that these lapses will not prevent those who use the term 'Christian Education' from continuing to reflect on what they mean by it.

Fred Hughes

To Viv, Alison and Karen

Contents

Abstract   9

1. The Background   11
2. Christian Education as a Particular Kind
    of Religious Education   39
3. Christian Education in Maintained
    Church Schools   53
4. Christian Education in Longstanding
    Independent Schools   66
5. Christian Education in Recently Established
    Christian Schools   73
6. Christian Education in the Church Context   92
7. Christian Education under Review   99
8. Relating the Concept Christian Education
    to County Schools   109

Appendix 1
The Religious Provisions of the Education Act,
1944 and the Education Reform Act 1988.   118
Appendix 2
List of Recently Established Christian Schools   123
Appendix 3
Further Extracts which Illustrate some of the
Thinking of those Involved in recently
established Christian Schools   132

References   133

Bibliography   153

Abstract

The first chapter introduces the theme of the book and explores the historical background and trends in society and education in and since the 1940s. Chapter two shows that the term 'Christian Education' has sometimes referred to a particular understanding of religious education. That usage is analysed and found to be unacceptable without significant qualifications.

The next four chapters clarify and analyse the understanding of the term Christian Education in four further contexts where it is used: Church schools (chapter three), longstanding independent schools (chapter four), recently established Christian schools (chapter five) and the education of people in the church context itself (chapter six).

Chapter seven considers the arguments Paul Hirst has made against the acceptability of the concept of Christian Education and contends that these arguments are not valid. This chapter also points out that the five contexts where the term Christian Education is used (as explored in chapters 2–6), do not include the county schools, except that the first usage explored was the religious education in county schools. In view of this the chapter maintains that it is important to explore the relationship of Christian values and principles to education in county schools, a task undertaken in the final chapter.

The last chapter asserts that Christian values and principles still have valid implications for education in county schools and that education based on these values and principles can legitimately be described as Christian Education. Aspects of a Christian view of creation and fallenness are used as illustrations and the possibility of relating a Christian view of redemption to education in county schools is also considered.

CHAPTER ONE

The Background

This book aims first to present a critical analysis of the various ways the concept of Christian Education is used and second to demonstrate the thesis that the phrase 'Christian Education' can have credibility when used to describe a possible relationship of Christian values and principles to the maintained sector of education in contemporary British society, including the county schools.

In an attempt to avoid misunderstanding, the phrase 'county school' is used throughout this book with the meaning it has in the Education Act 1944, where it refers to a primary or secondary school which is maintained by a local education authority and which was 'established by a local education authority or by a former authority'.[1] The phrase 'maintained schools' has a wider usage in that it includes both voluntary (mainly church) schools and county schools, since the voluntary schools are to a large extent 'maintained' through public funds. The phrase 'county school' may now be used in some educational discussions less often than was the case, particularly before the growth of comprehensive schools in the 1970s and 1980s. Between the passing of the Education Act 1944 and the increase in the number of comprehensive schools, many schools were called 'County Secondary' and some were called 'County Technical' schools. The term 'county school' is retained in this book because no alternative phrase is as precise. The term 'county school' is used in the Education Act 1986 and the Education Reform Act 1988.

Part of the background to the theme of this book is the tendency in recent decades to use the phrase 'Christian Education' to refer to contexts other than the county schools, which can give the impression that the concept is no longer relevant there. For example, the phrase is sometimes used with reference to independent schools with a Christian foundation. Hence, the task attempted first is the clarification of the various uses of the term 'Christian Education'. What follows is an exploration of the relationships between Christianity and education in county schools to ascertain whether the concept 'Christian Education' is any longer tenable when applied to the county schools. Instructive though it is to explore what Christian Education means in some independent schools, as over 93% of the nation's children are in maintained schools,[2] it is crucial to explore what, if anything, Christian Education can mean for county schools.

The central concern of this book is not the rationale for religious education. The focus is on the term 'Christian Education', which can be related to the whole of education not just to religious education. It is not that religious education is irrelevant, but that to concentrate on religious education would be to give too narrow a focus. There are therefore several key areas of interest in religious education, which are not explored here, for example, assessment and examinations in religious education, resources for multifaith teaching, supply of teachers. This does not mean that they are unimportant, but only that they are not at the heart of Christian Education.

Chapters 2 – 6 seek to analyse critically five somewhat different ways in which the concept of Christian Education is understood. There will be an attempt to ascertain what those who use the phrase mean by it and to identify any common or distinctive features in the spheres of usage. This clarification is necessary because the phrase is still used, with a variety of meanings implied but not often clearly explained. Chapters 7 and 8 seek to demonstrate and justify a continuing relationship between Christianity and education, with particular reference to the county schools.

The rest of this first chapter explores, in two parts, the background to educational discussions and developments since 1940. The first part summarizes relations between the Church and education in England, and the second summarizes some of the trends in society and the curriculum of English maintained schools. Some points are more immediately relevant to this exploration of Christian Education than others but developments in society and education are part of the background to the ways the phrase 'Christian Education' has been used since 1940 and have therefore to be kept in mind. The phrase had a context and usage in the 1940s and 1950s which cannot be ignored in any attempt to understand its changing context and usage in the 1980s and 1990s.

If there is suspicion today of the church's role in education, this should be no surprise when account is taken of the history of relations between the church and education in England both before and after the 1940s. For example, in 1919 when H.A.L. Fisher, the then President of the Board of Education, proposed 'that the control of all non-provided schools should be placed unreservedly in the hands of the local authorities, and that in return the authorities should be obliged to provide facilities for denominational instruction in all their schools at parents' request'[3] there was considerable resistance to this by many Roman Catholics, Anglicans and Nonconformists alike, as there also was to Fisher's plan to allow 'contracting out for those who insisted on denominational atmosphere schools'.[4]

Later, in 1930 and 1931, Sir Charles Trevelyan, the then President of the Board of Education, tried three times to get through parliament an Education Bill raising the school leaving age (his second attempt also included other proposals). At the first attempt the churches were not ready to commit themselves. The second attempt was resisted by Nonconformists and Roman Catholics. The third attempt, whilst supported by Anglicans and Roman

Catholics, was rejected by Nonconformists who felt that the proposals if adopted would enable the Anglicans and Roman Catholics to consolidate their position too much.

The desire for new initiatives, including new schools, continued and it took considerable negotiating skill and perseverance to get all the parties to accept the proposals contained in the Education Bill published December 1935, which led to the Education Act 1936. As a result of the Act, according to Marjorie Cruikshank, '519 proposals for new senior schools were submitted in the three years which were allowed, 289 by the Roman Catholics and 220 by the Anglicans.'[5] The outbreak of war in September 1939 prevented most of the proposals from materializing.

More could be said about this and one could go back even further, for example to the compromise worked out in the 1860s which, through the Education Act 1870, established the dual system by allowing the establishment of Board schools as well as the continuance of church schools. However, even this brief description is sufficient to indicate that when the early 1940s arrived there was already a long history of controversy surrounding the matter of the church and education in England, notwithstanding the considerable educational facilities provided by the church in the past centuries when the State's interest in education was very limited.

The British and Foreign School Society, closely associated with nonconformity, was established in 1808. It was then a focus for nonconformist participation in the provision of schools. In 1811 an Anglican society was founded: The National Society for Promoting the Education of the poor in the Principles of the Established Church. Starting in 1833 Parliament began making grants to these two societies but four fifths of the schools receiving grants were under Anglican control and the Nonconformists resented this unequal allocation of funds, especially as around half the population were not Anglicans.

Another nineteenth century development was the formation of the Ragged School Union in 1844 whose first president was Lord Shaftesbury (1801–1885). John Pounds had founded the first Ragged School in 1816 in Portsmouth. The Ragged Schools were for children in the cities whose parents were too poor to pay even the modest fees of the schools in the other two societies. The role of the Ragged Schools Movement changed with the passing of the Education Act 1870 bringing a consequent change of name to The Shaftesbury Society.

The Education Act 1902 allowed voluntary schools to be supported from the rates. Nonconformists objected to this, seeing it as 'religion on the rates'. Nonconformists also disliked the fact that in single school areas where the only school was Anglican, their children were more or less forced to attend an Anglican school. These factors largely explain why in this century Nonconformists have generally supported schools established by local authorities rather than church schools. The part played by Sunday Schools also needs mentioning. Though they concentrated on Bible reading and the teaching of Christian principles and morality, that was the only formal education many children had in the nineteenth century. The role of Sunday Schools arises again in chapter 6.

The factors that form the background to the Education Act 1944 are several and complex. The church had a large and longstanding part in the education system and wanted a religious element to continue in any expanded system, yet it could not meet unaided all the pressures for change, some of which came into stronger focus during the 1939–45 war. As previously, a way ahead could be found only through negotiation and co-operation.

The fact that controversies occurred, may not be the most significant factor for our understanding of religion and education in Britain. The fact that from the seventh to fifteenth or sixteenth centuries English education was in the hands of the church and 'knew no divorce between "religious" and "secular" education'[6] may be more significant. Commenting on this, even as late as 1963, Hilliard could refer to 'the conviction, never since lost, that religion is inescapably linked with education'.[7]

There are other aspects of the background to the Education Act 1944 which ought to be explored further. First, there is the large stake of the churches. Events leading to the passing of the Education Act 1944 cannot be fully understood without an appreciation of how large was the stake of the churches. In England, by the 1940s, the 'number of Roman Catholic schools had increased from 1000 to 1200 since the beginning of the century'.[8] Though the number of Anglican schools 'had fallen from 12,000 to 9,000'[9] in the same period, this was still a large number of schools and to them went 22% of the nation's children.[10] Overall, 'half the schools in the country were still church schools'.[11]

A second key to understanding the background to the Education Act 1944 is the need and desire for change that had arisen. This partly concerned the church school situation. Some action was necessary on account of the limited funds of the churches. For example, the quality of the premises of church schools was not as high as council school premises. When in 1925 the Board of Education published a list of schools with defective premises, the list had twice as many non-provided (ie church) schools on it as provided schools. Some of the defective premises were of course made worse in the two world wars.

Further, separate senior schools (recommended in the Hadow Report 1926) had 'been provided for 62% of senior pupils in council schools, but for only 16% of those in church schools'.[12] The Education Act 1936 permitted local authorities to make grants of between fifty and seventy-five per cent of the cost of new non-provided senior schools but the war prevented most of the building work being carried out. If these proposals had gone on to completion, they would have eased the financial burden on the church, but not solved the problem. As it was, a solution was still required.

However, in addition to such practical matters which obviously required attention, there was a widespread desire for change, arising from various factors, one being what might be called 'the other dual system'. The situation in which most pupils attended only elementary schools, whilst a minority were selected for secondary schools with superior resources and curriculum (and hence prospects) had come to be regarded as unjust, divisive and an unwise waste of talent. In 1946 Jeffreys wrote of 'our baneful heritage of elementary education — that is, an inferior kind of education, on the cheap, to give the labouring classes enough instruction to make them useful but not enough to put ideas into their heads'.[13] This situation could be remedied only by substantial change.

The war obviously influenced the nation as a whole, not least in its thinking about and desires concerning the future. Many people felt that Britain was opposed by forces intent on changing things beyond recognition. The preface to one book (dated 1st January 1940) said that England can not avoid 'the impact of forces which . . . have now deployed in strength upon mankind.'[14] In 1941, Livingstone expressed this vividly and dramatically:

Nazism, Communism and in a less degree Fascism . . . have more similarities than differences. They do not know the meaning of . . . Freedom . . . Justice, Mercy and Truth. . . . Suddenly .. the whole bottom has fallen out of our civilisation, and a change come over the whole world, which, if unchecked will transform it for generations.[15]

There was a strong consciousness that our way of life, the very nature of our society, was under threat, and that a new impetus and sense of purpose was necessary if our society, including its schools, were to preserve its values and strengthen its moral base.

Not only was there a desire to resist forces hostile to the nature of British society, but also a desire to do this by re-asserting the place of religion, or more specifically Christianity, in our society, including our schools. The Government White Paper *Educational Reconstruction* (1943) spoke of 'a very general wish, not confined to representatives of the Churches, that Religious Education should be given a more defined place in the life and work of the schools, springing from the desire to revive the spiritual and personal values in our society and in our national tradition'.[16] The basic assumption made by many in the 1940s was that Britain was a Christian country. It therefore followed that if the educational system of the country were to be revised, then it was appropriate for there to be 'Christian' religious and moral education.

The place given in the 1944 Act provisions to religious education in all maintained schools (including daily school worship and Anglican and Nonconformist participation in the devising of Agreed Syllabuses for religious instruction) partly explains why the churches accepted the Act. Some council schools had little or no religious instruction, though the Education Act 1870 allowed them to provide it. The Education Act 1944 offered the possibility of ending any tendency to confine education in council schools to secular subjects.

William Temple was one strong advocate of the relevance of religion for all schools. He said: 'Education is only adequate and worthy when it is itself religious . . . If the children are brought up to have an understanding of life in which, in fact, there is no reference to God, you cannot correct the effect of that by speaking about God for a certain period of the day. Therefore our ideal for the children of our country is the ideal of a truly Christian Education.'[17] That was in 1942. In 1943 he said: '. . . let us not give the impression that our concern as church people is only with the adjustment, of the dual system: we ought as Christians to be concerned about the whole of educational progress . . . .'.[18] From this point of view, the religious provisions of the 1944 Act were 'progress'.

However, some writers are cynical about aspects of the 1944 Act. For example, in 1987 Ralph Gower wrote:

> The bitter fact is that when Christians got together in the preamble to the 1944 Education Act, there was so little trust about the teaching of Christian faith and practice due to worries that there might be inter-denominational "sheep-stealing" that the most innocuous way of doing Religious Education was to teach children the Bible.[19]

It is important to note that though the Education Act 1944 does not specify that religious instruction and collective worship must be Christian, partly to avoid the possibility of courts having to decide what qualifies as 'Christian' religious instruction or worship, it was made clear in the debates in Parliament that Christian religious instruction and worship were intended. This point is taken up again in chapter 2.[20]

There have of course been developments since the

Education Act 1944. One obvious aspect is the nature of the task involved. In the House of Commons on 1st July 1946 the Rt. Hon. Ellen C. Wilkinson (Minister of Education), commenting on the task of implementing the Act, said 'As the Government interpret the Act, that task means no less than the overhaul of the entire system of State Education.'[21] She also said 'I want to emphasize that we want to educate children according to their ability and aptitude . . . I do not accept any idea that there ought to be different grades of secondary education.'[22] As will be explained below, considerable progress was made with this major task, but a review published in 1958 showed that the task was incomplete and a new initiative was needed.

A second development has been the raising of the school leaving age, first to 15 in April 1947. This had been recommended by the Hadow Report 1926 and provided for in the Education Act 1936. Then with effect from 1st September 1973 the school leaving age was raised to 16.

A third development has been the decline in number of church schools. Marjorie Cruickshank wrote that 'within a decade of the passing of the Act over a thousand village schools, the majority of them Anglican had disappeared completely'.[23] On 4th May 1950, in the House of Commons, R.A. Butler opened the education debate regretting 'the slaughter of the innocents in the shape of little country schools cut out of development plans by local authorities so that they are given no choice to opt whether to be aided or controlled . . .'.[24] Despite this decline, the church schools still form a significant part of the education system. Around 22% of school pupils in the public sector in England are in voluntary schools.[25] Further figures about the present situation are given below.

The Government White Paper *Secondary Education for All: A New Drive* (December 1958) summarized the remarkable growth in education since 1944:
— sixth forms in grammar schools : 'nearly doubled in size'.
— children staying on voluntarily beyond age of 15 years: 'up from 187,500 in 1948 to 290,600 in 1958'.
— full time students in Technical Colleges: 'risen from 47,000 to 76,000' over ten years.

— part time students in Technical Colleges: 'risen from 220,000 to 470,000' over ten years.
— number of university students: 'now double the pre-war figure'.
— school population of England and Wales: 'increase of well over a quarter'.
— new schools built: 'four thousand'.
— new school places brought into use: '2,000,000'
— number of teachers employed: 'risen by 85,000 since the war to a total of 260,000'.[26]

Clearly, although the number of Anglican schools had declined, there had been a notable post-war expansion in education at all levels. However, this White Paper also pointed out that the task of improving the provision of education was unfinished in some important respects:

> There are, today, too many children of approximately equal ability who are receiving their education in schools that differ widely both in quality, and in the range of courses they are able to provide . . . (Paragraph 10)
>
> There are still too many areas in which it has not yet been possible to give the secondary schools, and in particular the secondary modern, the resources that they need. And this is why many parents still believe that if their children go to a secondary modern school, they will not have a fair start in life. (Paragraph 11)[27]

The Paper therefore proposed a five year programme of school building (primary and secondary schools):

> As the first essential step the Government propose in co-operation with the local authorities and the Churches to launch and carry through a continuous building programme for primary and secondary schools covering the five years from 1960–61 to 1964–5. The value of projects started in 1960–61 will amount to fifty million pounds and in 1961–62 to about sixty million pounds. It will be the Government's aim to get work costing three hundred million pounds started in the five year period. (Paragraph 22)
>
> 'The main programme will be designed to complete the reorganisation of the remaining "all age schools". There are still about 150,000 pupils of eleven and over in these schools.' (Paragraph 24)[28]

With regard to religious education, the Church of England has continued to have influence. Various Anglican dioceses of the Church of England have often introduced new syllabuses for the church schools, and church representatives have actively taken part in conferences convened to prepare Agreed Syllabuses and in Standing Advisory Councils on Religious Education, when set up in accordance with section 29 of the Education Act 1944. In one notable case, the Church of England objected to an Agreed Syllabus adopted by a local education authority. This concerned the City of Birmingham Agreed Syllabus and the case is reported in *The Law of Education* by Taylor and Saunders[29] and in the British Humanist Association publication *Objective, Fair and Balanced*.[30]

The Birmingham Conference for the revision of the Agreed Syllabus, constituted in 1969, formally agreed a substantial 'Agreed Syllabus of Religious Education and Handbook of Suggestions for Teachers' on 28 January 1974. This document took the unprecedented step of admitting non-religious stances for living (Humanism and Communism) to consideration in their own right and not merely as subservient to religious instruction. This led to protest from the Conservative group on the Education Committee and the Bishop of Birmingham. Despite these protests the City's Education Committee formally accepted the document on 7 May 1974.

The inclusion of non-religious alternatives to religion represented a matter of principle which the religious opposition could not ignore. Before the next meeting of the Education Committee on 11 June, a legal opinion obtained by the National Society (Church of England) for Promoting Religious Education was made public. This was to the effect that the proposed Syllabus did not conform to the requirements of the Education Act 1944. The local education authority thus felt obliged to obtain its own legal advice, which confirmed the objection. In this situation, the Authority sought the advice of the Department of Education and Science, which advised that the Conference should be reconvened. This the Education Committee authorized on 8 October 1974.

There were two grounds for suggesting that the intended Syllabus was not acceptable legally. The first was that the Agreed Syllabus was only about 250 words long and was vague. Counsel for the City advised that certain sections were so vague as not to constitute a 'syllabus'. It appears that the six hundred page Handbook was more likely to shape school RE syllabuses than the extremely brief Agreed Syllabus. The second was that the 1944 Act required Religious Instruction, but the Syllabus and Handbook included substantial material on non-religious alternatives to religion. Counsel for the City advised that, though non-religious matters could be included in a syllabus of religious instruction, this could be done only if they advanced the instruction of religion and related to religious instruction and were not 'taught for their own sake'.[31]

The re-assembled conference extended the proposed Syllabus and heeded the legal warning on content, making appropriate changes. For example, on non-religious stances for living the revised documents say 'Such contextual studies contribute towards a critical appreciation of the distinctive features of religious faith' and the Introduction replaces the phrase 'stances for living' by the word 'religion' as in the following extract from the 1975 version: 'The syllabus should thus be used to enlarge and deepen the pupils' understanding of religion by studying world religions . . .' The revised Syllabus (1975) satisfies the legal requirements. The Church of England had demonstrated its continuing powers of influence.

In 1988, during the debates preceding the Education Reform Act, the Anglican and Roman Catholic churches sought to exert influence over the proposals to allow schools to opt out of the local education authority system.[32] The Act allows church aided and controlled schools to opt for grant maintained status.[33] There were objections from the churches, partly because if aided and controlled schools 'opt out' they could move further away from church control.[34]

The cost of the church schools to the churches continued to be high and at times their financial limitations were viewed favourably by Parliament. The Education Act 1953 'made grants available for building aided schools in new housing areas'.[35] The Education Act 1959 'extended a 75 per cent grant to all aided secondary schools, whether in existence or projected, which were built to cater for children at existing primary schools'.[36] Cruickshank shows that between 1945 and 1962 the Church of England had opened 215 new schools, approximately half 'controlled' and half 'aided', and the Roman Catholics 511 schools, none of them controlled schools.[37] In 1979 there was one Roman Catholic Controlled School — a primary school with 33 pupils.[38]

Overall, the number of Anglican schools had continued to fall (to 7976 in 1959 and to 6588 in 1969) and the number of Roman Catholic schools had continued to grow (to 2033 in 1959). By 1980 the number of Anglican schools had fallen to 5,488 and the number of Roman Catholic schools had risen to 2,525.[39]

Despite the reduction in the number of Anglican schools the stake of the church in education is still large. In 1980 a third of the maintained schools in England and Wales were church schools.[40] Also, at that time in England, one in every four primary children and one in six secondary children went to church schools.[41] This is a very significant number of children, but the twentieth century is one in which the proportion of children attending county schools has increased and the proportion of children attending Anglican schools has decreased:

Proportion of children in each type of school (%)

	1900	1938	1962	1967	1980
Council/County	47.0	69.6	77.6	76.9	78.0
C of E	40.2	22.1	11.9	11.8	10.9
Catholic	5.4	7.4	8.4	9.3	9.1
Other	7.4	0.9	2.1	2.0	2.0[42]

The nature of Anglican and Roman Catholic provision can be explored further.

In 1980, 64% of church primary schools were Anglican and 34% Roman Catholic. The secondary school figures show that Roman Catholics have put more resources into their secondary schools than the Church of England has:

24% of church secondary schools in 1980 were Anglican and 54% Roman Catholic.[43] This gap had narrowed marginally by 1985 but the general pattern remained. Social Trends 1987 said:

> Voluntary schools accounted for 23% of school pupils in the public sector in England in 1971 and 22% in 1985. There were 1,027 thousand pupils attending voluntary primary schools in 1985, 63% in Church of England schools, 35% in Roman Catholic schools and 2% in schools of other denominations and religions. In 1985, there were 608 thousand pupils in voluntary secondary schools, Roman Catholic schools accounting for 52%, Church of England schools for 25% and other denominational schools for 23%.[44]

A careful examination of all the figures shows that since the early 1960s the proportion of pupils in voluntary schools has remained around 22 to 23% but the actual number of pupils in them has increased: 902,000 in 1969, 915,000 in 1970 and 1,635,000 in 1985. During much of the same period the total number of pupils in the county schools was increasing too.

For over a century the Church of England has participated in the training of teachers. At the time the 1944 Education Act was passed, there were twenty-six Church of England Training Colleges[45] and they were seen as having a crucial contribution to make to the training of teachers, many of whom would help to give teaching in accordance with the new series of Agreed Syllabuses. Now the free-standing Church of England Colleges of Higher Education are reduced to eight. In 1986 the College of St. Mark and St. John, Plymouth was faced with the possibility of closure but was reprieved. It appears that the Church of England is extremely reluctant to allow any of its remaining colleges to be closed.

Other churches have also been involved in teacher training. For example, the Roman Catholic Church has seven colleges with teacher training courses. The Methodist Church has two colleges involved in teacher training: Westminster College, Oxford and Southlands College, Wimbledon (now part of the Roehampton Institute). West-hill College, Birmingham, an inter-denominational free church college, should also be mentioned in this context.

There have been criticisms of church schools from a small but vocal minority of people. These criticisms are usually that some church schools are discriminatory (socially, academically and/or racially) because of their admission policies, or that they refuse to co-operate with local authorities over falling rolls.[46] Admission according to parents' religion, often the first criterion for admission, obviously means selection of a particular kind. In some multi-racial areas especially, this policy is alleged to divide the community, as it results in there being a church school with mainly white pupils (some travelling from outside the immediate catchment area) and a maintained school with mainly 'coloured' pupils. It is difficult to ascertain all the facts but the case against church schools is quite well documented and some of the facts have been carefully obtained and recorded.[47] In July 1986, David Jenkins, the Bishop of Durham, said that in his view church schools were inappropriate in our plural society and ought to be phased out.[48]

In the summer of 1981, about twenty heads of Church of England secondary schools in London and the south-east produced the Allington Statement,[49] a brief document which urged, among other things, a closer relationship with local education authority policies on admissions and a sharing of the burden of falling rolls, a strengthening of diocesan powers over church schools in their dioceses, and a lessening of the powers of individual governing bodies. The Diocesan Boards of Education have been hesitant in embracing all the Allington recommendations. Somewhat disappointed with the response to its recommendations, the 1982 meeting of these heads issued, not a further statement, which they felt could easily be ignored, but a series of crucial questions which they felt needed urgent attention.[50]

Three other controversial aspects should at least be mentioned here. The first is the question whether public funds should be used to help establish and maintain schools for other minority religious groups, for example Moslems. In terms simply of equality of treatment, as there are church and Jewish schools which receive public funds, this should be extended to Moslems. Those who feel strongly that the existence of church schools is socially divisive are likely to think that extending financial support from public funds to additional religious groups could tend to reinforce division in society. This matter is raised again in chapter 3.

The second controversial issue is the matter of what precisely are the policies and intentions of the Labour Party, some leaders of which have at times appeared to favour the ending of the dual system (i.e. ending the status of voluntary or church schools partly financed from public funds) and the abolition of independent schools or at least the removal of privileges such as charitable status. On 23 March 1984 *The Times Educational Supplement* said 'Arguments for the freedom of parents to send their children to private schools were dismissed on Wednesday by Mr. Neil Kinnock . . . He attacked private schools for their effect on the maintained sector.' He was quoted as having said 'In a democratic exercise of freedom there is only one real border — the point at which its exercise by some individuals starts to impinge on the freedom of others.'[51]

The third controversial matter is the proposal of the National Society (Church of England) in March 1984 that some church school governors should give up their places to representatives of other faiths and that where a majority of children attending a church school are from other faiths, then the governing body should surrender its majority control for five to seven years. The first possibility, where a few governing places would be given up, is known as 'lend-lease governorships', and the second possibility as 'lend-lease schools'. It should be emphasized that the Green Paper which made these suggestions[52] was a discussion document and that the suggestions were for temporary, small-scale experiments. How those involved in church schools understand the concept Christian Education is explored in chapter 3.

The second part of this chapter explores some of the trends in society in the period since 1940 and their possible effects on the curriculum of English maintained schools. Gordon and Lawton, whilst trying 'to detect some important pressures in society which have reacted on the curriculum' take care to say that curriculum change is not 'determined by social events: there have often been individuals working in a counter-cyclical direction who have had a lasting influence . . .'[53] and that the 'connection between the prevailing social and educational ideas . . . and changes which take place in the curriculum . . . is a very complex one.'[54] Nevertheless, it appears to be true that changes in society have to some extent influenced education. Therefore, some of these are mentioned below. Though various factors are identified they overlap and interrelate.

The first major feature to be explored is the secularization of society and the accompanying revolution particularly in theology and religious education. An increase in secular tendencies was noted in a publication by the Department of Education and Science in 1971 which reported on a seminar organized by the former Secretary of State, Edward Short, and held in 1969. It stated that 'life is . . . more and more secular in a negative way.'[55]

Declining church attendance is often regarded as key evidence for secularization. Alasdair MacIntyre takes this view:

> If we look at what happened between 1900 and about 1950 in more detail we perhaps get some light upon the continuing causes of secularization. It is worth presenting the relevant figures in the form of percentages of the population rather than in numbers of members. It is only if one knows what proportion of those who might practise Christianity actually do that one can form a true conception of the extent of secularization. For the Church of England there is a decline between 1900 and 1950 in weekly attendance from eleven and a half per cent of the population to three and a half per cent.[56]

More recent figures are available. In the following example, secularization is not mentioned, but the general situation is clear:

> In the 1970s the British Church lost 1 million members,

closed 1,000 churches and lost 2,500 ministers. It was yet another decade of decline, when the Churches in England alone lost 0.68 million members. While the rate of decline lessened during the decade, all the mainline denominations continued to decline in membership. Therefore, any discussion of church growth must take place in the context of overall church decline.[57]

However, declining church attendance, whilst an illustration of secularization, is not an adequate account of it. Various writers have explored the complex nature of the concept. In his 1965 paper David Martin showed that the terms 'secular' and 'religious' are used in various ways and he maintained that 'there is no unitary process called "secularization" arising in reaction to a set of characteristics labelled "religious".'[58] Nevertheless, he accepted that there are 'certain broad tendencies towards secularization in industrial society', for example, 'that religious institutions are adversely affected to the extent that an area is dominated by heavy industry; that religious practice declines proportionately with the size of an urban concentration; that geographical and social mobility erodes stable religious communities organised on a territorial basis'.[59]

Bryan Wilson defined secularization as 'the process whereby (explicitly) religious thinking, practice and institutions lose social significance'.[60] Alasdair MacIntyre described some of the effects of industrialization on the working class, including their tendency not to attend church, but he also sought to demonstrate that they did not build up secular alternatives to religious and moral questions, and to explain why:

> A consistent and systematic secularism . . . depends upon the possession of a vocabulary by that group in which these questions can be asked and answered. Hence the loss of a framework and vocabulary by the English working class is itself perhaps the major inhibiting force which prevented secular views dominating them . . . instead there remains a strong vestigal Christianity . . .[61]

Some ideas about secularization are mistaken. David

Lyon refers to several, for example: 'that there was a "golden age" of faith, from which Western society has declined; that secularization happens automatically wherever "modernity" has arrived, without help from those who wish to speed it up and without regard to others who may try to resist it'.[62]

John McIntyre, though he is exploring the multi-faith nature of British society, takes issue with any assumption that Britain has had an exclusively Christian past which has recently been eroded:

> I should like briefly to note the error in assuming that British society was singularly monolithic before we had a great influx of immigrants. The values and concepts of Christianity which we have said constituted the ideological nucleus of western culture have been rarely without their critics in the past two hundred years. Western culture has scarcely ever enjoyed the security of the uni-faith situation; even in its hey-day of medieval Christendom, it was constantly under challenge from Islam. The situation is therefore not as novel as it is claimed to be.[63]

Though several writers seek to qualify claims about secularization and not to overstate them, or seek to give a comprehensive rather than simplistic account of it, they do not try to reject the word or deny altogether that there have been various tendencies which can loosely but reasonably be described as secularization, though it may have been less in some sections of society than in others. The fact that the term has sometimes been misunderstood, has sometimes been used simplistically and has had to be qualified in several ways, does not render it redundant. In 1965 David Martin said 'The word secularization is too closely linked to such distortions to be retained . . . Secularization should be erased from the sociological dictionary.'[64] Nevertheless, he has found it indispensable and uses it frequently in his 1978 book. Looking back to his 1965 paper he wrote 'I intended to open a debate rather than to banish a word . . .'[65] and David Lyon said 'It would be foolish to try to dispense with the term altogether.'[66]

Sociologists tend to study 'religion' in the sense that it

refers to 'the religion of the churches', 'official' or 'conventional' religion.[67] When used in this way, to refer to religious institutions or structures, it is difficult to deny that secularization has occurred, that is, decline in the activities and influence of the churches. It is in this sense that O.R. Johnston preferred to speak of a 'post-ecclesiastical society', rather than a 'post-Christian society'.[68] The significance of secularization is not so much in the symptom of declining church attendance, but in the decreasing church control of society, the decreasing influence of Christian institutions on views and decisions in public life, the tendency to answer fundamental questions without reference to religious or supernatural categories and the reduced attention given to Christianity in school.

This is not to say that secularization has been total, or that simply to describe Britain as a 'secular' society is adequate or correct. Nor is it to deny that the term secularization should be regarded as a 'problematic', by which is meant that 'secularization' is a term that holds various related matters together in a rather rudimentary and loose way.[69] Nor is it to deny that there are areas of vitality in religion, including Christianity, or that some of these are trying to resist tendencies towards secularization rather than to accommodate to them. It is however to maintain that the term still has some credibility and refers to changes which to some extent have actually happened. The word is used in the rest of this book within this context.

The tendency towards secularization involves particularly a changing attitude to Christianity and especially the relationship of Christianity to morality, politics and religious education and this will now be explored. To the extent that one of the intentions of the Education Act 1944, particularly regarding religious education, was to improve the moral quality of the nation, it was clear within twenty-five years of the passing of the Act that this was not being achieved. One publication expresses this as follows: '. . . we are faced today, on the one hand with criticism of the way in which religious instruction in schools is carried out, and on the other hand with evidence of the decline in moral standards. These two are inseparably connected.'[70]

All the same, not all the claimed results were felt to be retrograde. In 1962 results were published of 'A survey of the Day school and Sunday school relationship'.[71] Some of those responding from churches reported adversely on the effects of religious instruction and school worship as they saw them. The following are examples of such responses: 'It causes a decrease in Sunday school attendance'; 'It is a substitute — it inoculates children against Church worship'; 'It conditions children to think of religion as just another subject.'[72] However, some comments on the effects of religious instruction and school worship were more positive: 'The children are more knowledgeable, and therefore need more discussion'; 'Reverence is greater, and the children worship readily'; 'The Bible stories are better known'; 'Bible and hymn knowledge is increased.'[73]

Clearly it would be unwise to generalize on the basis of these statements, but they confirm that there were assertions that the religious clauses of the Education Act 1944 were not being implemented in a way that produced the moral improvements desired by many in the 1940s. Alongside this were fresh assertions that morality does not depend on religion.[74] The difference between the two realms could be argued theologically and philosophically, though with different emphases.

Edward Short wrote: '. . . today the idea of a code — providing for most people a ground-work of rules — has well nigh been replaced by the individual person using his own reason to decide what is "right" and "wrong".'[75] Short also wrote: 'The humanist and the agnostic believes he can live a perfectly good life without Christian belief — and of course he is right.'[76] A liberalizing of social norms was reflected in changes in the law regarding homosexuality, capital punishment, abortion, divorce, etc. J.W.D. Smith (1970) was in no doubt about the impetus for these changes: 'The tides of secular thought and life have swept away the familiar landmarks of moral standards and traditional belief.'[77] Further, it was a matter of observation that qualities such as toleration, kindness, generosity, honesty and patience were not the monopoly of Christians or religious believers, and there was a fear that if there is an insistence that morality depends on religion alone, then people who reject religious beliefs might feel they have little or no reason for acting morally.

At the time of the passing of the Education Act 1944 there appears to have been a widespread acceptance that democracy and Christianity were natural partners, both being regarded as accepted British belief stance, quite properly reflected in much British life, including school life. From at least the 1960s onwards, the assumption that democracy and Christianity are bound up together, each necessarily implying acceptance of the other, has been increasingly questioned. Though examples could be given of areas where rights and freedoms have been restricted, it is difficult to make a strong case that democratic principles have been seriously eroded.

Though it is correct to regard these changes as contributing to an increasing secularization of society, it must be remembered that Britain is not an entirely secular society. Some reasons for this position have already been given. Other reasons are the apparently frequent occurrences of 'religious experiences',[78] the contemporary interest in astrology and the occult, and the strong religious consciousness of some ethnic minorities. Having said this however, the fact remains that the questioning of the appropriateness of providing a Christian religious and moral education in the maintained schools of a plural society, provided the opportunities for a revolution in religious education and a generation of new moral education programmes, for example 'Lifeline', the materials from the Schools Council Project in Moral Education.[79] One factor that contributed to the declining interest in Christianity may well have been the prosperity of the 1950s, the 'you've never had it so good' era. When material prosperity looms large in a generation's aspirations and is attainable, a weakening interest in spiritual matters may be a more or less inevitable consequence.

Another factor contributing to the declining interest in Christianity and religion/religious education in general, is sometimes said to be the high status and regard given to science. For example, Sankey says:

> Within the western culture the advent of science appears to have gradually eroded the Christian view of man which for so long sustained it. Man is no longer seen as the special creation of God fondly formed from the dust of the earth and receiving His life-giving breath, but instead takes his place at the tail-end of the impersonal evolutionary process. He no longer stands at the centre of the Universe which was made for his benefit and delight, but is situated on a rocky planet which orbits a rather unexceptional star towards the edge of millions of galaxies. The sun and the moon are not the light bearing gifts for day and night and the rainbow is the result of diffracted light and not the sign of a divine covenant with men. In short these beautiful stories which stand at the beginning of the Bible have, for so large a proportion of the population, come to be of little more value than the stories about fairies and Father Christmas which were given up with childhood. And with that the whole edifice of Christianity has been seriously questioned.[80]

In theology and religious education there was a revolution during the 1960s. Edward Short wrote that the upsurge in radical theology was 'in its own way, as fundamental as the Reformation'. [81] That may have been an overstatement, but developments in the theological world helped to create a climate in which orthodox Christian beliefs were questioned more openly than in the war period and in the immediately post war years.

John Robinson was influenced by earlier writings, for example those of Paul Tillich. His *Honest to God* published in March 1963 and reprinted eleven times within two years, undoubtedly had wide popular impact in the United Kingdom. The Agreed Syllabuses of the 1940s and 1950s tended to assume the validity of the traditional view of the nature of God. The search for a Christianity which would be acceptable in the 'age of reason' involved a questioning of many of the traditional Christian views, and became known as 'radical theology'. It was given impetus in theological circles by theologians such as Bonhoeffer, Bultmann and Tillich, and in society in general by *Honest to God* and the ensuing debate.[82] The greater awareness of and sympathy with radical theology, had some influence on later Agreed Syllabuses and on religious education in schools. Some of these developments are described in *Teachers and the New Theology* by William Strawson.[83]

The findings and theories of notable researchers and writers had no less effect on religious education. The two key figures were Ronald Goldman[84] and Harold Loukes.[85] Their recommendation of a more 'child-centred' and less 'Bible centred' religious education and their outlines of religious development of children (stages of conceptual development broadly following the model of Jean Piaget) had a tremendous effect on religious education, an effect still felt today. The soundness of the research was questioned,[86] but Goldman's writings (more so than Loukes') became the new orthodoxy of the 1960s.

However, nothing stands still in religious education, and in the terminology of the 1970s and 1980s, Loukes and Goldman would be regarded as 'neo-confessionals'.[87] By the late 1960s the phenomenological approach to religious education was beginning to emerge, for example in: *Secular Education and the Logic of Religion* by Ninian Smart, 1968, and *Religious Education in a Secular Setting* by J.W.D. Smith, 1969.

In Schools Council Working Paper 36 *Religious Education in Secondary Schools* (1971), there are clear signs of Ninian Smart's influence. The phenomenological approach gained in popularity during the 1970s but has been criticized and so has been clarified and refined.[88] The nature of the 1960s revolution was documented in *Revolution in Religious Education: A Commentary* published in 1966[89] and was re-assessed by Edwin Cox in *Problems and Possibilities for Religious Education* published in 1983.[90]

A different trend to consider is the changing attitude to elitism, favouring egalitarian ideals instead, and particularly the expansion of comprehensive education. Though the Education Act 1944 required 'secondary education for all' and a kind of equality in education (for example, the supposed 'parity of esteem' of the parts of the tripartite system), the Act did not herald a common curriculum for secondary pupils across the land. Gordon and Lawton speak of the confused response of the Labour Party to the 1944 Act, notably in accepting the tripartite system so passively and for so long.[91] Equality of opportunity, even though unobtainable in entirety (if heredity gives anything that varies from child to child), was certainly not as great as it might have been.

The famous Circular 10/65[92] heralded much greater comprehensivization — Statistical Bulletin 6/84[93] shows that by January 1983 83.6% of pupils at maintained secondary schools were in comprehensive schools. *Social Trends 1988* puts the figure for England at 85.4% in 1986.[94] Growth in comprehensivization would inevitably mean fewer grammar schools and not surprisingly there was opposition. The Head of Watford Grammar School wrote in *The Essential Grammar School*, published in 1956, that he was afraid of 'death by drowning in the deep waters of the Comprehensive School'.[95] The Black Papers in the 1960s and 1970s[96] were largely a reaction to the push for comprehensivization. However, doubts about the accuracy of intelligence testing (usually the major factor in selection) were strengthened by research in the 1950s, especially concerning the extent to which social factors influenced results.[97]

Though Mrs. Thatcher withdrew Circular 10/65 when she was Secretary of State for Education, the Conservative Government has not implemented a reversal and is unlikely to do so, though the Assisted Places Scheme, the City Technical Colleges and the provisions to allow parents to opt for schools to be taken out of local authority control are looked upon by some people as indications of the limited Conservative confidence in comprehensive schools. The increase in the number of parents choosing independent schools for their children is sometimes alleged to be largely because of inadequate provision for the maintained schools under the Thatcher Government.

However, designating more schools as 'comprehensive' has not meant a common curriculum — differences between schools remain. Even the existence of core and foundation subjects, as required by the Education Reform

Act 1988, does not indicate a common syllabus for all pupils, and arguably ought not to do so, on account of the varying abilities of pupils.

All the same, in the last twenty years or so there has probably been more equality of opportunity than in the first twenty years after the 1944 Act. In one sense, equality of opportunity plainly did not occur while the tripartite system predominated. Now, in most comprehensive schools, all pupils have access to the same curriculum, at least in their first few years there, though some courses are followed only by pupils with particular abilities or aptitudes, for example, learning a second foreign language or tuition in a musical instrument. Offering pupils options for the last two years of compulsory education obviously means that once their choices come into effect some pupils will follow courses different from others. Also, the opportunities of boys and girls have become more similar — for example, many girls now take Craft, Design and Technology courses. Sometimes, a desire for greater equality has been regarded as an argument against the dual system, in that the church schools are seen by some people as preserving privileges for a minority of children.[98]

A further trend to mention is the technological revolution. Though there was in the 1940s an awareness of the need for a considered response to technological advance,[99] this awareness became heightened later. The needs of an increasingly technological society meant that the 1950s saw the beginning of new avenues of technical education. For example, the 1956 White Paper on Technical Education[100] led to the establishment of ten Colleges of Advanced Technology.

The demise of technical schools is against the general trend, though the number of technical schools set up as a result of the 1944 Act, was small. The impact of technology has been partly on teaching method, for example in the use of schools radio and television broadcasts, language laboratories, overhead projectors, videos, and computers. There has also been an effect on the content of the curriculum, for example the changed focus in Craft, Design and Technology courses already mentioned and in new computer studies courses.

Another way in which the growth in micro-electronics and automation has had implications for the school curriculum is in the need to prepare young people for the increased leisure time forced on many of them by unemployment.[101] This need to have 'education for leisure' has been one part of the impetus for 'life skills' courses. Another part has been the need to prepare pupils for employment in the high technology workplace. In such courses the matter of values is clearly important, for example regarding views about ambition, vocation and the purpose of life. Where there has been a tendency to provide life skills courses only for the 'less able' pupils, whilst the more able pursue academic courses, lifeskills courses have run the risk of being regarded as 'not really credible'. A continuing problem is the uncertainty about what pupils will do post sixteen — take up further study, training or employment, or become unemployed.

Increasing immigration had an effect on the school curriculum. In the 1960s, and into the 1970s, immigration into Britain was high compared to that in previous years. Between 1964 and 1968 the number of Asian Commonwealth citizens who immigrated into Britain was 142,600. This meant an increase in the number of pupils from Hindu, Moslem and Sikh backgrounds. In addition there were immigrants from the West Indies, who frequently came from a Christian background. The influence of immigration on religious education is discussed by Cox.[102] He said that teachers 'saw their task as explaining to their pupils the various religions to be found among them, and promoting understanding and tolerance. The aim was to help British born pupils understand the religions both of the indigenous population and of each other.'[103]

The response has matured in at least two respects. Firstly, now schools have in them many black and coloured pupils who were born in Britain, educational talk is rightly less of 'immigrants' and more of the 'ethnic minorities' and one outcome has been that teaching about various world religions is now often accepted as a basic part of the religious education of all pupils in every generation, not just as the initial response to immigration. Secondly, the more plural nature of our society (multi-cultural, multilingual, multi-racial, multi-religious) is influencing the broader school curriculum. Implications have been particularly felt in geography, history and English. Multicultural education is now a widely accepted concept, though it has taken on a more explicitly 'anti-racist' nature since the National Association for Multiracial Education changed its name to the National Anti-Racist Movement in Education.

The above trends in society have not been arranged in any order of priority and each of them could be explored in greater depth. Also, there have been other influences upon the curriculum which could be explored. For example, one could examine the role of the Schools Council and its successors the School Curriculum Development Committee and the Secondary Examinations Council[104] or of key Reports (for example, Crowther Report 1959, Newsom Report 1963, Plowden Report 1967, James Report 1972, Bullock Report 1975, Cockcroft Report 1982, Swann Report 1985).

Finally, it must be said that one would find it difficult if not impossible to demonstrate a direct relationship between trends in society and curriculum change. However, this is not to say that there is no relationship at all between the two or to imply that evidence for the relationship is not at any point strong. Clearly trends in society do influence the school curriculum, albeit mostly indirectly, though they are not the only or necessarily the greatest influence.

CHAPTER 2

Christian Education as a Particular Kind of Religious Education

The phrase 'Christian Education' is sometimes used to refer to a particular kind of religious education. This particular usage predominated in both county and voluntary schools up to and including the 1960s. Thus the Newsom Report 1963 said:

> The 1944 Act in its religious settlement was based on faith that these differences (between the Church of England and the Free Churches) could be resolved in such a way that they would not interfere with a real Christian education in county schools.[1]

The 1944 Act refers in sections 25–30 to religious education, religious instruction, collective worship and religious worship,[2] but, as was mentioned in chapter 1, it does not say that any of these should be Christian. Hansard shows that in the debates in parliament leading up to the Act it was thought unwise to specify 'Christian' religious education or instruction in the Act, although that was what was intended. That this was the intention is to some extent confirmed by the fact that the Act requires half of the members of the Agreed Syllabus conferences to be from the Church of England and other religious denominations (Fifth Schedule).

It is also confirmed by a clear statement made in the House of Lords by the Earl of Selborne that 'it is the intention of the Government and of the Bill that the religious instruction required to be given shall be Christian instruction, and that the corporate act of worship shall be an act of Christian worship . . .'.[3] The purpose the government had in mind was the strengthening of the moral and spiritual life of the nation.[4]

Accordingly, there was a tendency to assume that the religious instruction and worship would be and should be Christian. The way this was interpreted is illustrated by the various Agreed Syllabuses published between the 1940s and the 1960s. These largely contained biblical material. The City and County of Bristol Agreed Syllabus 1960 (also adopted in several other local education authorities, for example Essex) was one such syllabus and was entitled *Syllabus of Christian Education*. Another was the Northamptonshire Agreed Syllabus of Religious Education (Primary Section, 1968) which was entitled *Fullness of Life* and subtitled 'An exploration into Christian Faith for primary schools'. In the Foreword the authors said 'Our aim has been to teach our children, as our Lord did, to love God and our neighbours . . .'.[5]

Another reference to the general tendency to regard religious education in this way, is in the Introduction to one book which states:

> The tradition in religious education which was embodied in the first generation of post-war Agreed Syllabuses but drew upon earlier experience, sought to introduce children to the Christian way of life by introducing them to the Bible.[6]

Statements made in government publications in the 1960s can sometimes help to illustrate what was the prevailing view of religious education at the time. For example, the Newsom Report 1963 said:

> . . . no Christian could for a moment rest content with an education which brought men face to face with a crucifixion but not with Christ. Religious instruction in accordance

with any local education authority's agreed syllabus is instruction in the Christian religion.[7]

This association of religious education with Christian Education is discernible in the 1967 Report of the Special Committee appointed in 1964 by the Education Department of the British Council of Churches to consider the state and needs of religious education in county secondary schools.[8] This Report says: 'Religious education in the particular sense in county secondary schools is to be interpreted as Christian. It cannot effectively be anything else in our country.'[9] Colin Alves recorded the results of a survey commissioned by this Committee into religious education practice in secondary schools. He followed this with a chapter 'The New Approach Required'. Referring to 'major adverse factors in our developing situation which demand a reappraisal of the traditional methods and approaches of Christian education', he identified them as some of the 'reasons why RE is failing'.[10] The terms Christian Education and religious education appear to be used synonymously.

When Alves comes to the new approach outlined, he commends the practice of beginning religious education with current events and experiences rather than with particular past events. He goes on: 'In the Christian context this seems to imply beginning, for example, with an actual church building or with visible objects having religious associations: or with Sunday or festival day: or with a Bible, a book of worship, a hymn book: or with a service being enacted . . .'[11] The clear assumption is that pupils come from a Christian background or at least live in a Christian milieu.

The book asserts that 'preparation for church membership is the duty of the churches, not the schools'[12] and rejects religious education that 'smacks of indoctrination and proselytization'.[13] Nevertheless, the book implicitly sees religious education as Christian Education. The approach is different but the main aim still seems to be to bring pupils to Christian faith. The section introducing the new approach ends: 'Christian faith becomes real not through amassing and mastering any quantity of so-called facts of history, but rather through fostering the quest for meaning out of present experiences so that through the meeting life may be quickened and meaning revealed.'[14] Alves still commended syllabuses that had an almost entirely Christian content.[15]

A somewhat different expression of this attitude is Loukes' *Teenage Religion* (1961) where the approach to religious education is based on the discussion of problems and has four stages: raising the problem, analysis of the problem, the Christian judgment or interpretation, and application especially in the wider sphere of human relations.[16] He said this 'might be described as a Christian technique of problem-solving'.[17] What characterizes most researchers and writers on religious education in the 1960s is that whilst they recognized various failings in religious education in the past, they still thought of it as producing Christian faith, albeit through a more sophisticated, enlightened and somewhat more open approach.

A later book by Alves, which ranged more widely than religious education, entitled *The Christian in Education* is relevant.[18] Part of it was on religious education (chapter 3). Referring to the 1963 Newsom Report *Half our Future*[19] he described its chapter 'Spiritual and Moral Development' as displaying a clearly Christian standpoint.[20] Alves added 'that, at times at least, the Committee thought of themselves as Christians writing to Christians, and thought of religious education as making a direct contribution to Christian education. They also thought of Christian education as being quite specifically the task of the nation's schools.'[21] He went on to explore some aspects of the different kind of religious education that was emerging, for example, through the 1971 Schools Council Working Paper 36 *Religious Education in Secondary Schools*,[22] but the background Alves traced in his chapter on religious education again demonstrated the view that most religious education up to and including the 1960s was regarded as a kind of Christian Education.

Three aspects indicate the kind of religious education that predominated in the 1940s and 1950s and was commended in a more sophisticated style in the 1960s: a large amount of Bible study was still envisaged, a Christian response to matters facing pupils was assumed to be what the lessons should be directed towards, and the intention was still that pupils should come to adopt a Christian position. The following analysis explores the validity of interpreting Christian Education as this particular kind of religious education.

The term 'Christian Education' in the way it is used in these sources appears to involve a particular content (Christianity, especially the Bible), a particular viewpoint (a Christian view of the world, current issues etc.) and a particular intention (the emergence of Christian faith in the pupils). It would perhaps be easy to dismiss the view that religious education should be seen as Christian Education (in terms of content, stance and intention), as inappropriate in a multifaith society. Various reasons could be given for such a dismissal. Firstly, it is unjust, in view of the presence in schools of many pupils who do not come from Christian backgrounds. That is, it is not fair to assume pupils have a Christian background and then promote Christian religious education, in a school where such an assumption is false.

Secondly, it is not educationally justifiable and is likely to be counter-productive. That is, some pupils and parents will resent Christian assumptions being made, and a positive partnership between school and home is likely to be hard to maintain. Such resentment can lead to poor motivation and be detrimental to pupils' educational progress in terms of religious education and in other areas.

These arguments are strong, but other arguments have to be weighed against them. One such argument is that there appears to be some continuing desire for religious education to have a mainly Christian content. Some recent Agreed Syllabuses indicate this, though the aim may be different. For example, the Gloucestershire Agreed Syllabus 1981 says,

Although the context of religious education will vary from place to place, its content will be drawn largely from the study of Christianity in its many forms, this being the religious faith which has most influenced our culture.[23]

Some writers give much emphasis to Britain's Christian heritage and see this as a key reason for wanting Christianity to be the main content of religious education. Nigel Scotland is one such writer[24] and so are some of the contributors to the Order of Christian Unity publication *Curriculum Christianity.*[25] This publication arose from a conference in November 1976 at which various 'targets' were proposed and passed, one of which was, 'The conference would wish to see secured for the future a specifically Christian content of Religious Education in our State schools.'[26]

Another line of thinking that makes it impossible simply to dismiss equating religious education with Christian Education is the view that 'religion is inescapably linked with education'.[27] This view asserts first that education cannot be value free but can be only within a framework of values and a view of the nature of the world. However, it goes further and asserts that in Britain it is Christian values and the Christian view of the world that should form the basis of education, including religious education. The reasons given for this further assertion might be that Christianity has for centuries been the religion that has influenced and shaped British life or that those who make this assertion believe that there are good reasons for preferring Christian values to other values or that the Christian view of the world is correct.

It is true that education unavoidably involves views about the purpose of life and what are regarded as worthwhile activities. Besides such curriculum matters, the way the school is organized can at times indicate the value the institution gives to its various individual members. In this sense, the question of what values are at the roots of a school, is a crucial question. If the school is not to endorse Christian values in its religious education and in other areas of the school's life, the question remains as to what values will be endorsed.

However, the situation is not so simple, because a school can endorse some general Christian values without accepting the whole range of Christian beliefs. Nevertheless, it is possible to explore the degree to which a school seeks to divide its curriculum into religious and secular spheres or to see them as parts of a whole, as relating to each other or as being a somewhat false distinction. A school which wants to avoid making a strong distinction between the religious and the secular, if it has a Christian foundation or wishes in some way to commend Christian values and principles, may well want to provide a Christian kind of religious education in the sense in which that has been outlined in this chapter.

The close association of Christianity with education and religious education is different from the apparent separation between the secular instruction (s.23) and the religious instruction (s.25–30) of the Education Act 1944. However, this line of thinking is as much or more concerned with the overall basis of the whole of the curriculum as with religious education in particular.

The arguments against regarding religious education as Christian Education need to be further examined. The first mentioned was a moral argument — that it is unfair to give an education based on Christian assumptions to pupils whose basic assumptions, and whose parents' basic assumptions, are not Christian.

This argument may not be as strong as it sounds. In the first place, it must be said that many pupils and parents, whilst not being committed Christians, do not have a committed anti-Christian stance either. They might be described as agnostic, or as giving tacit acceptance to Christian principles and values. If they are agnostic they may be happy to accept a Christian religious education and see this as appropriate while their own uncertainty remains. The other parents and pupils mentioned are those who in their practice accept Christian principles and values, though with little if any personal Christian faith and without active participation in the life and worship of a local church. Their stance may be held somewhat subconsciously but if pressed their approval of Christian principles and values may make them express support for Christian religious education.

Pupils who are agnostic or tacitly accept Christian principles and values may appreciate the arguments about Britain's Christian heritage and be willing to explore Christianity. The parents may be as willing for their children to make this exploration. In this case, so long as there is no pressure to conform or to express Christian faith, both parents and pupils might well be happy with the content of religious education being mainly Christianity.

The second case to consider is the position of parents and perhaps pupils who have consciously come to convictions that are not Christian. They might be atheists or have a commitment to another religion. They may well object to the content and orientation of religious education being mainly Christian, however sensitively it is carried out. Their argument might be that such religious education is not in accordance with their wishes, perhaps because they see spending most of the religious education time on Christianity as a waste of time. This demonstrates the need to reconcile the desires of minorities and of individuals, with those of the majority.

In the 1960s there were many surveys about people's views on religion and religious education.[28] These tended to indicate majority support for retaining religious education. The kind of religious education preferred was usually unclear, but as most religious education in the 1960s was the Christian kind described in this chapter, it is perhaps reasonable to assume that the support was for this style of religious education. There appear to have been fewer such surveys in the 1970s and 1980s.[29] The results published by Souper, P.C. and Kay, W.K. in 1982 are about school assemblies in Hampshire[30] and one ought not to generalize on the basis of findings with such a limited scope.

However, if it is still true that the majority of people in Britain want religious education to be Christian Education, the position of those who do not want this should be safeguarded. The right of parents to withdraw their children from religious instruction and worship is some safeguard, though if it means an embarrassing marking out of a few pupils as different from their peers, that could be damaging for them and could be a somewhat high price to expect parents and pupils to pay. Also, it is no safeguard for pupils who would like to withdraw from religious instruction or worship or both and whose parents will not make the request.

Another safeguard may be the parental choice available

if different schools provide different kinds of religious education. A further possibility would be to allow parents the right to provide teachers to give the kind of religious education they wish in school during religious education time (cf the 'released time' arrangements in New Zealand and Australia, where 'special religious instruction' is taught by visiting clergy and other accredited nominees of religious groups). Section 25(5) of the 1944 Act is a possible safeguard as it gives local education authorities the power, in certain conditions, to allow pupils to be withdrawn from school during school hours in order to receive religious instruction elsewhere when arrangements for this have been made. If the provision of voluntary aided schools could be extended, that could offer additional choice and thus increase safeguards further. Some of these measures could be regarded by some people as giving institutional support for a divided and fragmented society. On the other hand, one could argue that recognizing the rights of minorities should be a key tenet in a plural society.

The proposals of the Swann Report[31] to extend the provision of phenomenological religious education and to remove the right of parents to withdraw their children from religious education, could be seen as a reduction in the recognition of the rights of parents who do not want their children to have this kind of religious education. At its best a phenomenological approach carefully seeks to clarify and understand the phenomena as understood by the participants but it is when categories of neutrality and objectivity are emphasized that some parents object to such an approach being enforced on their children, largely because in their view an adequate appreciation of a religion is not possible from the position of a detached observer alone.

The 1944 Act, by its requirement for local education authorities to devise Agreed Syllabuses for religious instruction, provided for regional variation. It is probably the case now that in some areas parents who want religious education to serve as Christian Education are in a minority.[32] The case for regarding religious education in maintained schools as Christian Education rests partly on the view that this is what the majority want. To that extent it is a pragmatic argument and always vulnerable to changes in popular opinion.

The second main argument mentioned against seeing religious education as Christian Education, was that it is not educationally justifiable and more specifically that it is detrimental to the educational progress of children who do not share the Christian assumptions. The first objection was that it is unjust as a matter of principle to have insufficient regard for those who do not hold a Christian position. This second objection is that there are educational arguments against it.

As with the first objection, it should be recognized that some parents and pupils, whilst not being committed Christians, are by no means against treating religious education as Christian Education and in fact may be happy to accept what is general custom. In that case, parental support can enhance educational progress rather than restrict it.

It could be said that the objection is not so much that regarding religious education as Christian Education directly limits educational progress for some children, but more that there is no educational argument to support it. This could hinge on whether 'what the majority want' is regarded as a valid argument. In the view of some philosophers, it would not be a valid argument, because they think educational policy should be based on what is rationally justifiable rather than only on what the majority want. One of the suggestions in this chapter has been that since education can not be value free, allowing education to be within the framework of values held by a substantial number of parents, does form a rational argument. As Britain is a society where value issues are controversial and where there is not agreement on some crucial value matters, that is a justification for having schools which, within limits, uphold a variety of value positions.

One further objection to regarding religious education as Christian Education is that the term religious education has been widely accepted as involving something far broader than Christian Education, in the sense of the content being mainly about Christianity, the framework being a Christian view of the world and the aim being the fostering of Christian faith. This wider view of religious education involves partly making no assumption that the main content should be Christianity. The influence of Christianity on British life is recognized as one valid factor, indicating that there should be some teaching about Christianity, but examples of other factors that should be regarded as relevant are, the various religions practised by many people in our society (for example between 1.5 and 2 million Moslems), the various religions that may be represented in a particular area (the school community itself, the immediate catchment area and the wider surrounding area), the resources available, the expertise of the religious education teachers, and the time available. Multifaith religious education not only has content broader than religious education that concentrates on Christianity, but it makes no assumptions about the truth of a Christian account of the world and does not see the development of Christian faith as an aim of religious education, though it may for some pupils be an acceptable outcome.

Regarding religious education as concentrating on Christianity may well have had widespread support in the 1940s and 1950s when coupled with this was a desire to see the religious and moral life of Britain revitalized. How widespread that support is now may be doubted. In this case treating religious education as Christian Education may be seen as appropriate for most pupils in a former era, but now not so appropriate for most pupils and not desired by as many parents as formerly. The more recent concept of religious education which, for example, seeks to help pupils understand the nature of religious beliefs and practices through exploring a number of religions and which is often called religious studies, reflects the struggle to secure a rationale for religious education which is educationally justifiable for and in practice acceptable to the majority of pupils.

Without denying the influence of Christianity in Britain, without exaggerating past Christian allegiance and without exaggerating the extent of secularization, it appears to be true that in some respects Britain is now less Christian than it once was. That was one of the contentions of chapter one. In this situation, one of the limits is the period in which regarding religious education as Christian Education for most pupils in the maintained schools can be justified or can have acceptance widespread enough to make it viable. There are regional variations and fluctuations of opinion within regions, and in some areas it might still be acceptable at the present time. If those with responsibility for religious education are in touch with local opinion, they will have some awareness of whether or not there continues to be substantial support for seeing religious education as Christian Education.

Some parents may well support religious education that has mainly Christian content, and even that tends to assume the veracity of a Christian view of the world, but they may not endorse the fostering of Christian faith or practice as one or the key aim. The Durham Report[33] did not use the phrase 'Christian Education' as referring to religious education and did not regard the fostering of Christian faith as a legitimate aim for religious education in the county schools, but it did still argue for religious education in county schools to have a mainly Christian content:

> . . . The content of the (RE) curriculum in this country should consist mainly of the exploration of the literature and beliefs of the Christian faith.[34]

British society is not monochrome. Modern Britain can be described as 'a somewhat secular society, with a residue of Christian values, with a minority Christian strand which is clear but diminishing, and also with other religious minority groups and activities, and also including those involved in the occult and astrology'. In a plural society such as this, many people do not want an overtly Christian religious education and it is then difficult to justify that being the kind of religious education offered to pupils in county schools. Those who try to preserve an overtly Christian religious education for all pupils, are likely to find many pupils and parents who have no 'heart' for it. That may be the biggest restraint on retaining Christian religious education in the maintained schools. Head teachers, local authority advisers, Her Majesty's Inspectors and others who have some responsibility for or interest in what happens, are another restraint. They may feel that in some schools an overtly Christian religious education does not help secure the support and co-operation of significant numbers of parents.

In the course of implementing the Education Reform Act 1988, in particular its requirement that new Agreed Syllabuses must 'reflect the fact that the religious traditions in Great Britain are in the main Christian whilst taking account of the teaching and practices of the other principal religions represented in Great Britain' (Section 83)), it is now clear that some head teachers, advisers and inspectors feel they are expected to foster a kind of religious education (and collective worship in schools) which they do not personally support.

The relationship of Christianity to education, including religious education, must always take account of the nature of a particular society at a particular time in history. Theoretical ideals can provide alternative models or visions to aspire to, but proposals always have to take realistic account of the current situation. In practice, there are parts of the country where with regard to county schools there is only limited support for religious education having mainly Christian content, for making Christian suppositions and for having the fostering of Christian faith as a major aim. If Christianity does have implications for religious education in places where people do not want it to be synonymous with Christian religious education, then different implications will have to be elucidated.[35]

In voluntary schools with a church or Christian foundation, seeing religious education as Christian Education in the sense explained in this chapter, is more justifiable and advisable[36] than in schools which have no such foundation. However, even in these schools, an education that gives pupils no help in understanding the major non-Christian religions represented in our society, can reasonably be described as an inadequate preparation for their life in British society as it now is. It would be possible for a school to have religious education, conceived of in this broader way, in addition to the Christian religious education which has a more narrow scope and purpose.

The main conclusion of this chapter is that it is not justifiable to understand Christian Education as a particular kind of religious education appropriate for all county schools in contemporary Britain. The religious education needed must be wider in scope. The wishes of some pupils and parents must be considered. However, it may still be justifiable in some areas and some county schools, with qualifications — notably about providing in addition a broader religious education, perhaps in parts of the curriculum distinct from the Christian religious education. The latter might be called 'confessional' religious education and the former 'non-confessional' religious education but as Rossiter asserts these are somewhat unsatisfactory terms because they are 'opposite by definition'.[37] He prefers the terms 'education in faith' and 'education in religion' and commends a dialectical relationship between them.[38] In a school with two kinds of religious education the question of the relationships between the two would be crucial. Those involved in church schools might feel that 'education in faith' is the more important of the two tasks and this question arises in the next chapter.

In the task of understanding the concept of 'Christian Education', it needs to be noted that its general meaning, as used in the context explored in this chapter, is a particular kind of religious education (not the broader curriculum or process) and that it indicates a mainly Christian content, a Christian perception, and the fostering of Christian faith.

CHAPTER 3

Christian Education in Maintained Church Schools

The Church of England has a dual concern for education. On the one hand there is a desire to provide through its church schools something of particular value for the children in its churches — sometimes referred to as its 'domestic' educational task.[1] On the other hand it feels concern for the general education of the whole community. Anglican schools may help it serve the whole community, but concern for the whole community includes also interest in county schools.

This attitude has its origins in the time when the two functions were combined in the educational provision the Church of England made before the State began to be financially involved. The first government grant for schools in England and Wales was in 1833. This was a grant to the British and Foreign School Society and the National Society. Prior to this, and while State involvement remained minimal, the Church of England was able to see its 'domestic' and 'general' interests in education as one.

The first grant of State aid for Roman Catholic schools was in 1847. Traditionally, Roman Catholic schools have regarded their schools as providing for Catholic children, but unlike Anglicans have not sought provision of or involvement in education for the whole community. This stance has been widened somewhat, partly by the establishment of ecumenical or 'shared' schools[2] and by calls for Catholic schools to develop a broader role in the community. For example, an article in *The Tablet* in 1983 says: '. . . the Catholic school should fulfil an unprecedented function in the human community. There should be a profound ecumenical character to its selection of pupils, its curriculum, its ethos and its readiness to meet the varying needs of the local community.'[3]

The use of government funds in church schools has increased[4] and since 1870 many non-church schools have been established. Whilst the proportion of children attending Anglican schools dropped from 40.2% in 1900 to 10.9% in 1980, the proportion attending county schools rose from 47% to 78% in the same period.[5] Though the number of Anglican schools has been reduced,[6] the church-state partnership has been perpetuated and church school provision continues to be substantial.[7]

However, arguments have been raised against church schools from both within and outside the churches. For example, some argue that the pupil intake includes a disproportionately large number of more able children and a disproportionately small number of pupils with behaviour problems.[8] This itself may not be intentional but a consequence of entry policies which give first priority to children whose parents are active members of the particular church to which the school belongs and high priority to children from other Christian denominations.[9]

Another allegation is that church schools have been unwilling to co-operate with local authorities on falling rolls.[10] To an extent there are church secondary schools which admit children from church families who live some distance away rather than non-church families who live closer to the school.[11] One group alleges that 'in some areas church schools have become white enclaves using religion as a means of discrimination'.[12] Where church schools have a number of West Indian pupils (as they often come from Christian families) this allegation is clearly not entirely true. A policy which includes some pupils and thus excludes others on the grounds of their religious background is in a sense discriminatory, but not directly on the basis of skin colour or racial origin.

In some church schools it is possible to meet both the demands for places by those actively involved in the church and the demand for places made by others, but where church schools are oversubscribed and the pupils admitted are those with the strongest church links, the selection is plainly on the basis of a religious criterion. Allegations of improper discrimination are not necessarily justifiable. Discrimination is not necessarily morally wrong, though the word 'discrimination' is often used in a pejorative way. In education the word is sometimes used with a meaning that is not pejorative at all.

For example, the thinking behind the General Certificate of Secondary Education includes an understanding of 'differentiated assessment' and one explanation of this concept says that 'All examinations must be designed in such a way as to ensure proper discrimination so that candidates across the ability range are given opportunities to demonstrate their knowledge, abilities and achievements — that is, to show what they know, understand and can do.'[13] The assertion here is that discrimination in this sense is vital in the interests of the equitable educational treatment of pupils. Another example could arise from the fact that though there has been an increase in the integration of handicapped children in ordinary schools (since the Education Act 1981), some special schools still exist and this could be said to constitute a discrimination between pupils. If the pupils who attend special schools receive there a more appropriate education than is possible in other schools, this discrimination is morally and educationally justifiable for that reason.

These examples show that any allegation of wrongful discrimination in the admission policies of church schools has to be justified. It might be claimed that since there are church schools which exclude some children whose parents would like them to be admitted, this discrimination is unfair because it denies to some pupils something desirable and arguably better than alternatives, and should be removed by the closure of church schools with the more equal treatment that would result. However, even if this included closing all independent schools, a degree of discrimination would remain and could be increased, since some popular county schools are already oversubscribed and consequently a number of pupils are denied places, so closing church schools would increase this oversubscription in some cases and hence increase the number of cases where the desire of parents for places has to be denied.

There may be some scope for enlarging the popular schools, but the possibility that demand will exceed supply will always remain and with it the necessity for discrimination in who is admitted and who is not. A further noteworthy consequence of closing church schools is that doing so would be at the price of denying to some parents the right to have their children educated in accordance with their religious views and there is a good case for saying that this right should not be sacrificed.

Selection at least partly on the basis of religious background may be justified because the church invests in church schools partly to provide a particular kind of education for its children and this may be more appropriate for children whose parents actively support in the home what is offered in the school than for those whose non-christian background might make this active support significantly more difficult to obtain. Against this is the view that a policy which secures an actual or apparent privilege for some pupils at the expense of others is unjust and to that extent unchristian. On the other hand, in a democracy one of the valued rights is, or ought to be, for parents (as stated in the *Universal Declaration of Human Rights* 1948 'to choose the kind of education that shall be given to their children'.[14]

Clearly, there are constraints on what can be chosen. The nature of the world often limits the choices possible. For the sake of illustration, suppose parents in London came to regard one particular school as 'the best' and all parents in London wished to send their children to this school. It would be physically impossible for all these children to attend this school, but the right to express a preference and the obligation to meet it when reasonably possible[15] are justified in the present situation because there are various views about what is the best kind of education and this continues to be a controversial question.

In such a situation it is morally wrong to impose only one kind of education when it is possible to allow more than one. Where a variety of alternatives are actually available, there is genuine respect for human rights.

However, parents do not have an absolute right, regardless of what it is they want or regardless of the views and wishes of other interested parties such as the State. While this caveat takes account of the fact that often there are competing rights and interests, it should not be taken as indicating that the right can be easily dispensed with or that there is no genuine right at all. The assertion that parents have some rights is based on a particular view of the nature of humanity in which fairly high value is placed on family life and the role of parents. This area is further considered in chapter 5.[16]

The kind of education provided in church schools could be in jeopardy if there were an insistence on open access. O'Keeffe found that five under-subscribed Anglican aided primary schools in her sample 'accepted pupils if their parents agreed that the acceptance of a place for their child was tacit acceptance too of the Christian life of the school'.[17] If there were open access with no understanding that parents would generally support the kind of education provided in the school, they could work to undermine it. Whilst any undertaking given by parents when their child is admitted could be rescinded, that is no reason why church schools should not explain to parents the support the school hopes parents will give and seek to secure such support.

Important characteristics of church schools are discussed later in this chapter[18] and if a substantial number of parents were actively to oppose these the health of the school could be weakened. For example, if a number of parents campaigned to reduce the place of Christianity in religious education or to minimize church-school links, such a campaign, if it were successful, could fundamentally change the kind of education provided in the school.

The point here is that Christian parents, and others who support what church schools offer, have a right to preserve in church schools the education they want for their children. Only if there is a clear case of children being

abused or damaged in the school should this right of
parents be curtailed. This is because children themselves
have certain rights, for example to protection from ill-
treatment. If parents are allowed the right to have their
children educated in accordance with their religious
position, there is almost certainly bound to be a variety of
kinds of schools. One can make this a basis for an
accusation of unacceptable discrimination or divisiveness
only if one is willing to deny the right of parents to choose
the kind of education to be given to their children.
Vigilance in preserving this right, for Christians and
others, could be regarded as a just and therefore Christian
response.

Making education in church schools available to children of only some parents is not a denial of the right of
other parents to support a different kind of education for
their children. In defending this right for Christian parents
there is an implicit acknowledgement that other parents
also have this right. Any parent who objects to the right
of some parents to have their children educated in church
schools whilst seeking to retain their own right to have
their children educated as they wish is being inconsistent.
Sometimes the demand for places in church schools is
greater than the number of places available. This is particularly true at secondary level since the Church of
England has provided fewer secondary than primary
places.[19] That is perhaps an argument for increased support for church schools from public funds or for non-
church schools to give closer attention to what parents
want, but it can hardly be adequate grounds for changing
what church schools provide or reducing the number of
church schools which provide it.

There have been attempts to obtain aided status for
some Moslem schools. The debate about this is not crucial
to the nature of the education provided in church schools,
but is mentioned because it is a related question and there
is a prima facie case for saying that if there is to be justice
then there is no reason why in principle the advantages
of aided status should be denied to Moslems whilst being
offered to others. It is not that Christian parents have the
right to have their children educated in accordance with

their religious convictions and that Moslem parents do not. It is rather a debate about whether in carrying out this task both groups are entitled to the financial and other benefits which aided status brings.

Reluctance to give aided status to some Moslem schools may be for various reasons. There is a concern that what is offered in Moslem schools and what would continue if aided status were granted could be better described as 'indoctrination' than as education in the way it is often understood in contemporary British society with its emphasis, for example, on developing rational autonomy. However, in the case of church schools, concerns about the nature of the education being provided have not prevented the granting of aided status and it seems unfair to invoke that now as a reason for refusing aided status to Moslem schools.

Another concern is for the welfare of girls in Moslem schools. There is a view that the role of women in Islam is more restricting on their freedom and opportunities than is thought right by many people in contemporary British society. Most Moslems, of course, deny that in Islam women have inferior status and freedom, but the allegation is definitely made. A further concern is that if aided status is granted to Moslem schools this perhaps increases the likelihood that other religious groups will subsequently request the same status for their schools and the whole trend would harmfully deepen divisions in society.

The issues raised so far in this chapter set the background for an analysis of the nature of the Christian Education understood to be available in the maintained church schools. They may not all relate directly to what these church schools are providing but, by illustrating that their very existence and some of their practices are provocative elements in a number of controversial areas, they demonstrate the importance of attempting to clarify how those involved in these church schools understand the Christian Education they are seeking to offer.

Proponents of church schools mention various features of the education which church schools seek to provide. These features interrelate in the life of the church school and can not be separated out, but they can nevertheless be identified for the purpose of clarification. To some extent these features may be easier to maintain in aided schools than in controlled schools. In aided schools the governors have some powers that the governors of controlled schools do not have. For example, the general position has been that in aided schools the teaching staff, including the Head Teacher, are appointed by the governors and religious allegiance may be taken into account, while in controlled schools the teaching staff are appointed by the local education authority in consultation with the governors but no enquiry on religious allegiance is permitted. In some cases 'local management of schools' is changing this somewhat. Obviously the precise situation varies from school to school and some controlled schools may exhibit these features more than some particular aided schools. This could be demonstrated only by particular cases.

One feature often mentioned is ethos.[20] This may be what one writer calls 'a Christian atmosphere'.[21] This is rather a general notion but some idea of its meaning may be ascertained from considering some of the main characteristics of church schools.

Often the worship in the church school is thought to be highly important. There is some evidence[22] that church school assemblies are more explicitly Christian than those in county schools. Because the government acknowledged that some of the provisions of the 1944 Education Act concerning collective worship were not being followed in many schools, it proposed modest changes in the law regarding collective worship, for example to relax the obligation that it has to be at the start of the school day and has to be a single act of worship.[23] These amendments were enacted in the Education Reform Act 1988. John Hull's book *School Worship: An Obituary* [24] asserts that there are several reasons why worship in county schools is not justifiable. The doubts about the justifiability of having worship in schools appear to have led to the demise of worship more in county schools than in church schools. It may well be that in church schools more parents and pupils expect and accept that there will be

worship and the concern that they are not giving voluntary assent to it is less justified than in county schools
which, unlike church schools, often make no assumptions
in favour of Christianity.

Sometimes the 'sacramental life' of the school is mentioned as part of the worship in church schools.[25] Sometimes a communion service is held on the school premises
and sometimes in the local church. In church primary
schools it is usually only the adults who receive the
elements, but in church secondary schools they are sometimes received by pupils who have been confirmed or who
are full members of another Christian denomination. Even
when few or no pupils receive the elements, it is regarded
as important for pupils to witness this aspect of worship
and be involved to some extent. It demonstrates an
affinity between worship in the church and worship in the
school.

Attention is sometimes drawn to the religious education
in the church school. One document refers to 'the emphasis that is given to R.E. in voluntary denominational
schools'.[26] Another mentions 'the continuing right to
teach Christianity' [27] as if that is what is intended in the
religious education in the church school. The National
Society *Manual for Church Schools* in a section headed 'The
school and the local church' says:

> The school is not the place for narrow evangelism (the
> children can't escape), but the teachers should be aware of
> their responsibility to share with their children the truths
> which they have discovered, and to share their beliefs. This
> is an immensely tender area and should be approached
> with humility and care.[28]

The majority of syllabuses for religious education in aided
church schools contain only Christian material, often
based on the Christian calendar. There is an exception in
a recent document about religious education in Church of
England voluntary aided primary schools in the Diocese
of Chester.[29] It maintains a basically Christian framework
but inserts features of other religions where they can link
fairly naturally with the Christian content. For example,

in a section about practical Christianity it is suggested that reference might be made to Zakat (charitable giving in Islam).

For the church school the appointment of staff is of particular importance. This means appointing what one writer calls the 'right people'.[30] Burgess is more explicit: '. . . in the aided school the managers can — and for the most part do — earnestly seek to appoint men and women of Christian conviction.'[31] These comments show that there is sometimes an awareness that to a very large extent it is the staff who are in a position to influence the life of the school. Without Christian staff it might well be difficult for a Christian ethos to be fostered in the school. This is not to say that Christian teachers always play their part perfectly or to deny that teachers who are not practising Christians sometimes make a valuable contribution to the life of a church school. It is to assert that Christian teachers may have more inclination and concern than others to support and foster some characteristics thought to be important in church schools, for example the worship.

The first of two major characteristics of church schools given by Alves, is 'the close presence of an adult community'.[32] He means a Christian community, sometimes a monastic community, but mostly the Christians in the local church. Ideally, there will be close links between the church and its church school. Clergy may be involved in religious education, including school worship. Pupils and staff may visit the church as part of their religious education course and for worship, for example at some Christian festivals or for a Leavers' Service. Sometimes the church school premises are used for church purposes, for example a Sunday School, when the school is not in session and this can add to the awareness that the church and its church school belong together.

There is sometimes in church schools an attempt to allow Christian principles and practice to influence every aspect of the school's life including what is taught in lessons. A recent Gloucester diocese document *Worship in Church of England Primary Schools* asserts that worship 'should have direct links with the curriculum and should be central to the whole life of the school'.[33] Burgess thinks that among the aspects thought to be important, 'Christian parents would emphasize . . . the teaching of all subjects from the angle of Christian faith and morality.'[34] He may be somewhat optimistic when he goes on to say, 'Christians inevitably approach all subjects they teach in the light of their personal convictions.'[35]

A document published by the Southwark Diocesan Board of Education refers to the 'prophetic element' in the work of church schools.[36] Sometimes the church school should help pupils to question some of the values currently advocated by some sections of society. This is the same as the second major characteristic Alves advocates for the church school when he refers to its attempts to make its own critique of society. He expresses this as follows:

> . . . if society is in need of God's redemption, then the Church schools should be hoping to send out young men and women who do not conform to society's standards, but are prepared to challenge them — constructively but uncompromisingly. The only way to achieve this is by creating within and around the Church school a community which is markedly better than society in general.[37]

Alves overstates his case when he asserts that this is the 'only way' to help children learn to challenge society's standards. Certainly a church school can attempt to have in its community relationships of mutual care, respect and tolerance and especially compassion for those who are deprived or handicapped, and this experience of relationships may make a lasting impression on pupils. Then if they find that some relationships lack these qualities they may recognize this and seek improvements. However, the situation is complex and there are other ways of learning besides experiencing relationships of quality. A church school ought not to imply that there are no standards in society to which pupils should conform. Rather pupils should be helped to discriminate between the varying standards and values they could embrace. Careful thinking about moral questions is vital here and the use of case studies, for example, can help in this process.

It is sometimes thought that church schools should be

particularly interested in maintaining close links with parents. Cooperation between home and school can be beneficial in a child's development in a way that confrontation or indifference cannot. Also there may be theological reasons for having a high regard for parents and families. The National Society Manual states: 'Increasingly the school and home must be seen as a partnership.'[38] In Burgess' view since in aided schools the incumbent is often chairman of the governors he should seek opportunities to explain to parents 'the benefits of a Christian education in a Christian community'.[39]

Some, but not many, of those who write about church schools mention as important the school's attitude to its pupils. Noel Todd asserted that 'there are specifically Christian insights into how to deal with children'.[40] He said these included the place of sanctions, necessary because of the human condition. Bernadette O'Keefe suggests that church schools are popular because of their 'good discipline'.[41]

Other characteristics are sometimes attributed to church schools.[42] Those already mentioned here serve to illustrate much of what is usually thought to be important about church schools. It should not be thought that all of these characteristics are peculiar to church schools. For example, many county schools seek to maintain close links with parents and to regard the educational task as a partnership. The county school may also encourage some questioning of the values prevailing in society, though it might give different reasons for doing this. However, recognizing that some county schools seek to share some of the features of church schools need not and should not mean that they should be denied by church schools, though it does mean that such schools may not have good reason for claiming that those features make them distinctive from county schools.

Anyone conversant with education in church schools who uses the phrase 'Christian Education' with reference to church schools, is likely to have had that understanding of Christian Education moulded by these characteristics, some or all of which they will have observed in the church schools within their experience. It is difficult to summarize these characteristics and to describe briefly the ethos of church schools, but they clearly do involve the school's staff, its curriculum especially the religious education and including the worship, its links with the church and parents, and its attitudes to society. These demonstrate that when the phrase 'Christian Education' is used to apply to what is provided in church schools it is a very comprehensive concept.

Since many church schools, especially church secondary schools, give first priority to children of Anglican parents and second priority to those of other Christian traditions,[43] this influences the school's composition and hence may have implications for the kind of Christian Education attempted. For example, religious education and school worship that is more overtly Christian may be thought to be more appropriate than would be the case if more non-Christian pupils were in these schools. This policy could emphasize the church's 'domestic' concern for education at the expense of its claimed general concern for the education of the wider community, though it must be remembered that some church schools have a considerable number of non-Christian pupils.[44]

Paul Hirst has been a frequent critic of the kind of education attempted in church schools.[45] He regards education as aiming at 'the basic development of children as autonomous rational beings'.[46] According to Hirst this is a 'sophisticated' view of education, whereas a society that 'seeks to pass on to the next generation its beliefs and values'[47] has a 'primitive' view of education. He asserts that this 'primitive and unacceptable'[48] form of Christian Education is what denominational schools have in the past been concerned with and recommends them to distinguish between 'the two distinct activities of education and catechesis'.[49] Hirst's views in this area have been challenged[50] and will be analysed in chapter 7.

CHAPTER 4

Christian Education in Longstanding Independent Schools

It is appropriate to start this chapter in the same way as the Durham Report starts its chapter on religious education in independent schools.[1] It recognizes that the proportion of pupils in independent schools is small compared with those in maintained schools and yet that the term 'independent schools' 'covers a bewildering variety of educational institutions'.[2] In view of this wide variety, this chapter does not attempt a comprehensive description of the different kinds of independent school but is confined to an attempt to analyse the expression 'Christian Education' in so far as it applies to independent schools.

Whilst a detailed historical examination is not appropriate here, the origin of some of the independent schools is relevant. Some are associated with ancient cathedrals. Of these King's School, Canterbury 'may date from the year 598',[3] King's School, Rochester is purported to have been founded in 604 and there is evidence that St. Peter's School, York was founded in 625.[4] That links between Christianity and education go back to such early times partly explains why there has traditionally been a key place for Christianity in independent schools. Edwards expresses this as follows:

Education was at the heart of the Christian mission to

England. We should expect that St. Augustine would place the establishment of a Church school among his first priorities and what evidence there is suggests that Christian education in Canterbury is very nearly as old as the Archbishopric.[5]

The leading public schools were founded later, for example Westminster and Winchester in the fourteenth century and Eton in the fifteenth century. Thomas Arnold became Headmaster of Rugby in 1828 and fostered education that would produce 'Christians, gentlemen and scholars — in that order'.[6] Some of the schools founded in the nineteenth century and influenced by the Arnold tradition were the Woodard schools, founded by Nathaniel Woodard (1810–1891), the first of which was Lancing College in 1848. In the 1980s the Woodard schools have been reviewing their raison d'etre and this work is considered later in this chapter.

With this long history of Christian involvement in independent schools it is no surprise that 'Ecclesiastical dignitaries are usually found on the governing bodies of independent schools'[7] and that Christian activities continue to be part of the life of many independent schools. Dancy states clearly: 'The traditional instruments of Christian education are three: the chapel, scripture teaching and the general influence of the community.'[8]

Some aspects of many independent schools are different from those of most maintained schools. To begin with there is a considerable boarding element, which makes it easier to have house prayers, house communions and evening prayers. Boarding staff can be in loco parentis to a degree hardly possible for maintained school staff. Many independent schools have a full time chaplain on the staff[9] and many have their own chapel.[10] There is a tradition of preparing pupils for confirmation and this is scarcely possible or necessary for schools in the maintained sector. There is some evidence of decline in the number of pupils being confirmed.[11] Some independent schools make attendance at regular worship compulsory but some are experimenting by making attendance voluntary at most services.[12]

The variety of kinds of independent schools, mentioned

at the start of this chapter, should of course be remembered. Some schools have no boarders and some have only a few. Some have no chapel and some have nowhere large enough to take the whole school.[13] Some have class and house assemblies, and in some independent schools there are days when no kind of assembly is held.[14]

In general it may be true that a greater religious observance is expected in independent schools than in maintained schools. In independent schools there is no statutory right of withdrawal from religious education or religious worship, and in many the religious activities tend to be greater in number and more integral to the life of the school than is the case in most maintained schools. This virtual compulsion and the monotony many pupils profess to find in the worship[15] lead to some resentment, but there are attempts to improve quality, partly by having a degree of variety, spontaneity and pupil participation.

Traditionally many independent schools have thought of themselves as seeking to create a Christian community. Where attendance at Christian worship is mainly voluntary and some pupils opt out, it would be incorrect to regard the Christian community as 'co-extensive with the school'.[16] However, that is not the only possible model for a Christian community. When a compassionate and caring attitude is demonstrated by those who regularly participate in the Christian activities, towards those who do not, that can be regarded as a key criterion in the creating of a Christian community, rather than conformity by all the school's members.

References to a particular ethos seem to be fewer in the literature about independent schools than in that about church schools in the maintained sector. This might be because the place of chapel and scripture teaching is so fundamental that the ethos this creates is obvious and scarcely needs mention. However, it is sometimes mentioned. The Carlisle report has a section on independent schools[17] and refers to independent schools that are 'aiming at a Christian ethos'.[18] Dancy uses the word 'atmosphere' and appears to have something at least akin to ethos in mind:

. . . religion is caught, not taught; the faith of any particular boy depends less on the ordering of the chapel services or the scripture teaching than on the general religious atmosphere of the community . . . This general atmosphere depends ultimately upon the headmaster and the Chaplain.[19]

The Woodard Corporation now maintains twenty-five schools and various others are associated with it.[20] In 1984 and 1985 the Woodard schools carried out a review of their aims and ideals. The paper produced at the end of that process gives the following as the intention of Nathaniel Woodard and of the Corporation and its schools: 'that young people shall be taught Christian faith and practice in accordance with the tradition of the Church of England as it is contained in the Prayer Books'.[21] The same paper says this purpose today includes three aims. They are quoted here in full because they are comprehensive and further abbreviation could easily omit an important ingredient.

1. That each pupil shall be Christianly educated within the tradition of the Church of England, thereby achieving his or her full potential as a child of God, understanding the nature and importance of Christian faith, sharing in regular Christian worship, prayer and sacramental life and discovering the meaning of Christian vocation in the world.
2. That Woodard Schools shall express a specific educational idea, namely the provision of a learning community in which different aspects of knowledge and culture are seen as part of a coherent whole. Woodard schools are to base their educational programme on the Christian view of man and the world and to carry it out in a community founded on Christian principles and led by the Spirit of God.
3. That each pupil shall be given the opportunity to develop his or her talents to the full within the context of a lively school community combining the best of traditional and contemporary methods of instruction and a wide range of extra curricular activities.[22]

Stated like this it is clear that the Christian Education envisaged is intended to engender Christian religious practice and a Christian view of the world. The Woodard paper regards compulsory attendance at some services of worship as justifiable 'because the aims of a Woodard school are here made explicit'.[23] It is such convictions that led Basil Mitchell to assert that there must be an element of nurture in a Christian Education.[24]

There has been a debate about the nature of nurture and education.[25] They have often been seen as distinct processes but there have recently been attempts to show that there is a false dichotomy in the way they are sometimes understood.[26] One of the key aspects is the concept of education that one has in mind. This crucially affects the question of whether or not nurture is antithetical to education. This chapter thus comes to the same point as chapter three.[27] Hirst's views about the definite difference between education and catechesis apply as much to independent schools seeking to provide a Christian Education as they do to church schools in the maintained sector. Chapter 7 explores some of the points made by Hirst.

Some comparison is now possible between the nature of Christian Education attempted in church schools in the maintained sector and that attempted in the independent sector. Both sectors seek a particular ethos and both see the head teacher as crucial in establishing and maintaining this. This does not mean they necessarily seek an identical ethos. Worship and sacramental life appear to be key features of many independent schools and maintained church schools, though the extent of these is probably greater in independent schools especially where there are a substantial number of boarders or where a chaplain is on the staff or where both are the case.

In the many independent schools where the chaplain teaches scripture, there is likely to be a large place for Christianity in the syllabus. The same can be said of the religious education syllabus in church schools.[28] As far as staff are concerned, independent schools tend to appoint people who were themselves educated in independent schools and who may therefore be aware of the Christian traditions often present and who may be at least sympathetic to them. A similar affinity is sought in maintained church schools with varying degrees of success.[29]

The last chapter indicated that there is some desire for maintained church schools to explore a Christian view of subject content. The Woodard statement already referred to shows that sometimes in independent schools there is an intention to develop a 'Christian view of man and the world'[30] though this is much easier to express as an intention than it is to carry out in practice. This difficulty has also been experienced in many of the new wave of Christian schools established in the 1980s and this is considered further in the next chapter.[31]

Two features of maintained church schools would be much more difficult to implement in independent schools and therefore appear to receive little mention. One is the close links with a local Christian church. Where a school has its own chapel and probably Sunday services, there may be less need or inclination for close links with a local church. This may not be the case with independent day schools, that is those with no boarding pupils or very few. It is not the case with every independent school that has boarders.[32] Much depends on the effort that is made to develop links.

Another feature that can be difficult for many independent schools to implement is close links with parents. That is not to say that no attempts are made to maintain as close links as possible. It is to suggest that at least with boarders close links with parents are in practice often difficult to maintain most of the time.

A gap between what is intended in independent schools and what actually happens is sometimes admitted. Goodliffe acknowledged with reference to confirmation services that 'parents could not easily come over'[33] and remarks that 'however genuinely sincere the candidates may be, after even one or two years the majority will become lapsed communicants'.[34]

Dancy recognizes a gap with regard to religious education: 'No such gap between intention and achievement is likely to be greater than that in the matter of religious education. But the intention is at least something, and it is present both in the constitution of most public schools and in the hearts of most of their headmasters.'[35] From the point of view of the intention of the founders it is probably important to keep the main intentions alive even if fulfilling them is difficult. Possibly many parents and pupils are aware of this and other gaps, but prefer there to be efforts to reduce the gaps rather than to abandon the intentions.

With the generally high emphasis on chapel and scripture it may be more or less inevitable that a sizeable proportion of pupils acquiesce for the sake of appearances whilst at heart remaining cynical or indifferent. One of the early Bloxham Project publications acknowledged this: 'There may develop a certain conformity to Christianity, as part of a general conformity to school life, but little inner commitment.'[36] This is a gap of another kind. If conformity without sincerity receives even tacit approval, that could amount to a damaging endorsement of hypocrisy, though probably motives are rarely if ever perfectly sincere and the relative degrees of 'mere conformity' and sincerity can never be completely accurately quantified.

There are suggestions that the role of chapel and scripture has been more for maintaining social order than for encouraging genuine Christian faith.[37] This tendency is not confined to independent schools. In society at large there is considerable participation in church activities such as those related to rites of passage (eg weddings and funerals) and those related to major festivals (eg Christmas, Easter, harvest) and a very plausible account of this can be made in terms of conformity to social custom rather than of personal Christian faith and allegiance.[38]

CHAPTER 5

Christian Education in Recently Established Christian Schools

This chapter is first a brief description of the recent growth of new kinds of Christian Schools in Britain, identifying in particular the ways in which those involved in these schools understand the Christian Education they are seeking to provide, and second a critical evaluation of the main features of Christian Education as it is understood in this context.

There have been various developments and groupings in the recent growth of the Christian Schools movement, a growth which has gained momentum in the 1980s. One organization involved is the Christian Parent-Teacher League (CPTL), founded in 1966. It has the following aims:

a) to form a link between persons interested in the Christian doctrine of education and its implementation.

b) to stimulate, publicise and circulate opinion on Christian education by magazines and meetings.

c) to research into and provide information about the legal, financial and practical requirements regarding the founding of independent Christian schools.

d) to form a link between parent-controlled Christian day-schools, when established and to provide non-controlling help to the establishment of such schools conforming to the reformed standards.[1]

CPTL publishes a regular *Newsletter*. The December 1980 issue reported on meetings on Christian Schools in Wales in June 1980 to which about 35 people came and in Perth in September 1980 to which about 40 people came and on a conference on Christian Schools held at Drayton Green in October 1980, convened by Ian Murray-Watson to which about 40 people came.[2] The Winter 1982 issue reported on a Christian Schools conference held in March 1982 at Stapleford House Education Centre, Nottingham under the auspices of the Association of Christian Teachers and the Summer 1983 issue reported on a further Christian Schools conference, again at Stapleford House in March 1983. These conferences indicate the interest there was in Christian Schools in the early 1980s. CPTL favours parent-controlled Christian schools, rather than schools controlled by local churches. One aspect of the work of CPTL has been to give encouragement and advice to Christian parents who are educating their children at home or are considering doing so. Sometimes, as more likeminded parents have been linked up, Christian Schools have developed out of these home education groups.

A different development has been the establishment of schools which use the Accelerated Christian Education materials, produced in America. These are programmed learning materials. Emmanuel Christian School, Fleetwood, established in 1979, was the first school in Britain to use this scheme. ACE favours schools controlled by local churches.

A number of 'King's Schools' have used these materials, for example those in Basingstoke, Harpenden (formerly at Garston and Hemel Hempstead), Southampton and Witney. They have been linked together and since 1983 have organized Christian Education conferences (about 300 attended the Bristol Conference in 1987) and starting in 1984 published the *King's Educational Supplement*. Under their auspices were the Association of Christian Schools' Heads and Christian Schools Advisory Services, both founded in 1984. CSAS closed down in July 1987 but hoped to resume its work. CSAS produced and published Individualised Programme Learning materials (IPL) which are based on similar principles to those of the ACE materials but have content more appropriate to the British situation. Though CPTL was established earlier than the King's Schools and their associated organizations, these latter have been more active.

Around sixty Christian schools started in the 1980s, for example Acorn School, Romford, Essex (founded 1980); The King's School, Witney, Oxon (founded 1984); Oak Hill School, Bristol (founded 1984); The River School, Worcester (founded 1985). A fuller list of these recently established Christian schools is in Appendix 2.

The CPTL Newsletters and The King's Educational Supplements indicate that these recently established Christian schools have frequently encountered similar problems, for example with premises, finance, and HMI visits/reports and DES registration.[3] These are not explored here because the first concern in this book is the analysis of the way the concept of 'Christian Education' is understood, not the exploration of the practical problems encountered. Therefore the following discussion is an exploration of the understanding of Christian Education, which those involved appear to have.

In explanations of why particular Christian schools started, two main motivating factors are frequently mentioned. Firstly, there was (and still is) a conviction that there is a biblical injunction upon parents to bring up their children in the 'training and instruction of the Lord' (Ephesians 6:4) and that Christian schools are needed to fulfil this. The education in Christian schools is seen as being done on behalf of the Christian parents because of the view that biblically the responsibility for the upbringing of children, including education, lies with the parents. It often involves them in the school and sometimes activities deliberately take place in the home during the normal school day. One writer, referring to parents of Covenant School Stockport (opened 1981), wrote: 'We see the school as an educational extension of the home.'[4]

Secondly there was the view that many maintained schools were deficient in ways that made them unacceptable to some Christian parents. Hence, these Christian schools profess to attempt to give pupils a different overall 'message' from that communicated through the county schools, that is 'Christian' rather than 'humanist' or 'secular'. This presumably also involves helping pupils themselves to come to the view that much of British society including the schools is humanist and secular. Sometimes church schools within the maintained sector and independent schools with a Christian foundation have also been regarded as deficient. The view has been that many of these also have surrendered too much to secular humanist influences. There are sometimes other motivating factors, for example a conviction that education ought not to be one of the functions of the State. The following extracts illustrate these points (further extracts are quoted in Appendix 3).

The curriculum's

. . . appeal will be to those parents who do not want an atheistic, materialistic or permissive education for their children . . .[5]

The real question is whether we should allow our children to be taught at all in schools where the whole system of education ignores and contradicts the Word of God.[6]

If you would not allow blasphemy or obscenity in your home, why is it permissible to send your child to a school where such things are common?[7]

An educational system needs a clear and powerful view of life to guide it. The clear and powerful view of life that our civilisation gives us is that life is meaningless, nothing is really good or bad, and that nobody can erect standards and values that have relevance to anyone but himself. Our society is doggedly agnostic; and so no God can be allowed to give us a frame of reference to guide social aims and structures . . . An agreement on a clear standard is simply impossible at present. . . . Perhaps positive Christian action along a new line will give a lead to those confused and demoralized teachers so pathetically jammed in the dark tunnel into which humanistic thought has led British education.[8]

. . . the generally poor quality of education within the borough . . . was forcing many people to examine what sort of schools they would want their children to go to. . . . it became clear that God had never put the provision of education within the realm of the state's responsibility. Responsibility in this area rests squarely with the parents and then with those to whom they feel happy delegating this portion of their children's upbringing.[9]

There are two main assertions that emerge from these extracts and need to be analysed. The first is that biblically the responsibility for the upbringing of children, and therefore for education, is with parents, and the implication that to fulfil this responsibility home education or Christian schools are needed. Reference is frequently made to Deuteronomy 6, Ephesians 6:4 and to various proverbs, for example Proverbs 22:6, 'Train up a child in the way he should go, and when he is old he will not depart from it.' Perhaps the key section in Deuteronomy 6 (shortly after the giving of the ten commandments) is verses 6 and 7: 'And these words which I command you this day shall be upon your heart; and you shall teach them diligently to your children . . .'. The emphasis on these passages can be simplistic. Other relevant biblical material is considered later in this chapter. The second assertion is that most maintained schools are now based on humanist assumptions, the effects of which are harmful to children and can not be tolerated by Christian parents. These will be analysed in that order.

Since Deuteronomy 6 is often quoted in literature about Christian schools, this analysis will start there. As biblical support is claimed for the function attributed to parents, one has to explore whether it is sound as an interpretation of the biblical material overall. Hebrew parents were told to teach their children three things. The first was to obey all the commandments (for example those in Deuteronomy 5), to keep them and do them (cf.6:1f). The second was to love God with all their heart, soul and might (Deuteronomy 6:4).[10] Thirdly, parents were expected to tell their children what God had done in the past (Deut.6.20–25).[11] One could summarize these by saying that Hebrew parents were told to give spiritual instruction and moral instruction. Some proverbs illustrate these two facets. For example, in Proverbs 23:15–26 the son is told to 'continue in the fear of the Lord' (v.17), to be truthful (v.23), and not to be greedy (v.20) or drunk (v.21).

Three further responsibilities of parents can be distinguished. The first is to control and correct their children (i.e. discipline). This is clear from both the Old and New Testaments.[12] The second is to care for and love their children. This is regarded as fundamental and normal.[13] The third, an aspect of the second, is to provide for their children's needs, for example, food and clothing.[14] However, the responsibilities and authority of parents are not total — their rights and responsibilities are limited. There are various reasons for saying this.

Firstly, biblically, the children are God's gift, as for example in Psalm 127:3: 'Lo, sons are a heritage from the Lord.' He created them and gives them and they first belong to him. In this sense parents are answerable to God and ought not to say or act as if 'our children are ours to do as we like with'. The responsibility of parents not to provoke their children is clear in the New Testament[15] and must be kept in balance with the responsibility of children themselves which is mentioned in the next paragraph.

The second reason for asserting that parents do not have the sole responsibility in their children's development is that biblically, children themselves bear some responsibility for their actions.[16] This implies that the onus is not exclusively on the parents. The fifth commandment, 'Honour your father and your mother', plainly applies to children as well as adults. The New Testament confirms this position, for example in Ephesians 6:1–3 and Colossians. 3:20. The Old Testament sometimes makes it clear that if a child persists in rebellion he bears the responsibility himself and is punished.[17] Deuteronomy 21 shows that parents were told to take a rebellious son to the elders — parents were not allowed to mete out capital punishment themselves.

A third point to mention is that God is the only absolute authority. Parents should not re-shape his decrees. For example, if they command their children to steal or lie or cease to pray, the child is not obliged to obey as he is responsible to a higher authority.

A fourth argument to consider is that some responsibilities, though genuine, are shared. To assert that parents have responsibilities for the upbringing of their children, is not to say that they alone are responsible. This point will be explored further below.

A fifth reason for not placing responsibility for the upbringing and education of children exclusively on parents is that in practice few if any parents can actually teach their children everything they need to learn. The areas of knowledge are now so wide that parents cannot hope personally to instruct their children in everything. Also some of the skills children need to develop may not be ones the parents can teach. Only a hermeneutical approach that is naive would allow direct transfer, unqualified, from the position of parents 1200 or more years BC to that of British parents in the 1980s and 1990s. Nevertheless, a general principle may be clear and legitimate, though its application in practice be a matter for debate and variety.

This analysis suggests that to say, 'Parents alone are responsible for the upbringing and education of their children', is not to tell the whole story. It does not take note of all that the Bible teaches. The Bible does give parents much direct responsibility for giving their children spiritual and moral instruction, but that is not to say that parents also have a direct responsibility to teach them matters like maths, science or geography. However, this does not mean that Christian parents need have no interest in what happens in the teaching of such subjects. Some educationalists, for example Paul Hirst and Richard Peters,[18] have pointed out that it is not enough to teach isolated pieces of information — pupils must be helped to develop a coherent picture, to relate the parts to each other within the whole picture, to see each item in context.

Christians should be very interested in this process for at least two reasons. Firstly, a biblical view of the world, derived from its teaching on the sovereignty of God, is that the whole universe is God's: he created it, keeps it in being and nothing is outside his oversight.[19] This means that Christians should not 'compartmentalize' as if some areas of knowledge are secure in a world of their own, shielded from influence by a Christian or other world view. In principle, Christian beliefs give a view of the world which is not entirely the same as that which other beliefs give. Therefore Christian parents should be very interested in the picture of knowledge and the world which their children are developing.

Parents may not be competent to teach the details of chemistry or history or whatever (this is not to suggest that Christians have different formulae or results in chemistry or different dates for events in history) but when it comes to seeing the meaning and significance of each part in relation to the whole,[20] then a Christian view is distinctive and Christian parents do have some responsibility for teaching their children a Christian view of the world. David Lyon said:

> The scope of Christian claims on the whole spectrum of life is shrivelled as soon as a relative autonomy is granted to politics, economics or technology. Once Christians succumb to the view that such spheres should operate only according to their own internal criteria, they have in fact surrendered to secularity themselves.[21]

The second reason for saying that Christian parents rightly have some interest in what is taught in every area of the curriculum, is their desire for themselves and their children to love God with all their heart, soul, mind and strength (Mark 12:30) and to be those who by redemption through Christ are having their minds renewed (Ephesians 4:23). In other words, a Christian's convictions should not be shed as redundant when he or she comes to science or literature or any other subject. Rather, they should remember their Christian beliefs and seek to ascertain what insights they give to each subject. This task may sharpen the responsibilities of parents. It is possible to take account of this, whilst not accepting that all the responsibility lies with parents or that parents' responsibilities can be fulfilled only through Christian schools.

It is necessary to explore briefly the role attributed to the State in the Bible, as this indicates a source of interest and responsibility to put alongside that of parents. There are two key New Testament passages[22] and in these four functions of the State can be detected. The first is to punish the wrongdoer (Romans 13:3f). The second is to levy taxes (Romans 13:6f). The third is to praise those who do right (1 Peter 2:14) and the fourth is to administer justice. Acts 16:35–40 and 25:8–11 bring out the State's responsibility to protect the innocent.

These verses do not refer just to central government. 1 Peter 2:13f refers to 'every human institution, whether it be the emperor as supreme or to governors sent by him'. It is legitimate to regard teachers in the maintained schools as one branch of the State's rightful authority, 'in loco civitatis' as well as 'in loco parentis'. They are, in fact, local government employees and in some respects agents or representatives of the State. They share in the task of maintaining and upholding law and order; they have a legitimate function (in a limited sphere) of administering justice, punishing wrongdoers and praising those who do right. They themselves of course are also subject to authority — though not anyone's puppets.

Local and central government services exist for or on behalf of the people — for their good and not for some other end. Employees of both central and local government have sometimes rightly been called 'public servants'. This means that seeing teachers and schools as partly agents of the State is not to alienate them from the people — even financially the teachers and schools are provided for by parents via taxes and rates.

The State's role is not total or exclusive any more than the parents' role is. It is possible for monarchs and other national and local leaders to go beyond their powers and this is acknowledged in the Bible.[23] It therefore follows that the role of teachers is limited. They are to help children acquire knowledge, understanding and skills, but they ought not to use their lessons to inculcate in a morally unjustifiable manner a particular religious or world view, though they need not pretend that they do not have views of their own or be afraid of explaining them when appropriate or imagine that pupils will not develop some world view or other. This sensitivity to each child is required partly on account of the nature of the child. Children are vulnerable and impressionable and should be helped voluntarily to develop their own religious views, rather than have their options closed by the manipulation of teachers or other adults. The meaning and relevance of children being in the image of God is explored in chapter 8.

It is also necessary to explore briefly the role of the church. In the Old Testament era much teaching was in the Hebrew home, sometimes in a room set apart for it. Later it was associated with the synagogues and the temple. The aim was to enable people to read the Old Testament, to understand it and to live according to it. Mothers taught daughters about womanhood and domestic skills. Fathers taught their children their occupation. The Old Testament illustrates a principle of involvement of both parents and religious leaders in the upbringing and teaching of children, but again one should beware of making inappropriate transfers from the Old Testament situation to that of the present day.

Some early Christians allowed their children to have a secular education. The Christian Church had a particular concern for training church members and leaders. The church's interest in education for all children increased in the nineteenth century and paved the way for greater provision for education to be made by the State.

The point here is that Christian churches have a legitimate and continuing role in teaching Christian adults and children (see chapter 6). The precise involvement of children in the early churches is not clear from the New Testament, but it seems likely that they had a place and learned a lot from their involvement. Some at least of Paul's letters were passed round and read in various churches[24] and some parts of his letters were addressed particularly to children[25] so it seems highly probable that they were expected to be present. In the light of Jesus' own practice and teaching[26] children could hardly be denied a place in each Christian community. The point to note in this present context is that the church has a legitimate role in the teaching of children. The responsibilities of Christian parents for their children are not such as to prohibit a contribution from the local church though, as with the State, the church's role is limited. One task for Christian parents is to explore the part the church can play and endeavour to balance the church's contribution with their own contribution.

In summary, it can be said that the Bible gives parents particular responsibilities in relation to their children, but some responsibility is also given to the child, the State, and the church, though none of these has absolute authority or total responsibility. It is a relationship of trust, with a healthy ebb and flow of care and concern. If any one group tries to assert total or exclusive rights, it goes beyond its authority. If teachers say to parents: 'Keep out — what happens here is not your business', they deny the parents' legitimate interest. If parents say: 'You will do with my child in school or church precisely and only what I say you may', they begin to claim absolute authority.

We have here, not a simple line management situation (God — parents — children) but a more complex situation, an intricate web of relationships, in which parents, children, teachers and sometimes the church are involved, though the greatest burden of responsibility is on the parents. Part of this process can be examined by exploring the concept of teachers being 'in loco parentis'. It is not embodied in any statute. Rather, it rests on common law, and has been shaped by case law.[27] In Williams v Eady (1893) Mr. Justice Cave defined a schoolmaster's duty as follows: 'The schoolmaster is bound to take such care of his boys as a careful father would take of his boys.'[28] The definition was quoted by Lord Esher, then Master of the Rolls, who added that there could not be a better definition of schoolmaster. Barrell and Partington say that 'Mr. Justice Cave's statement is still the most used definition of a teacher's duty and is usually cited in cases where teachers are accused of neglect.'[29]

This century the courts have occasionally amplified and strengthened the 1893 definition. For example, in Beaumont v Surrey County Council 1968 (a case arising from an injury to a boy's eye during morning break) Mr. Justice Geoffrey Lane said: 'The duty of a headmaster towards his pupils is said to be to take such care of them as a reasonable, careful and prudent father would take of his own children.'[30]

The concept has been further shaped by one piece of recent legislation, the Education Act 1986, through which corporal punishment is prohibited in maintained schools (since August 1987). This does not apply to independent schools. Those who maintain that reasonable parents at times use appropriate corporal punishment and that teachers (being 'in loco parentis') should have the right to do so too, are likely to feel that the extent to which the concept now applies in maintained schools has been eroded. Of course, the view of some parents in our society is that reasonable parents never use corporal punishment. In an article entitled 'Kingdom Education' Peter Davis wrote: '. . . the school will stand by and uphold the parents and in a real sense act "in loco parentis".'[31] It appears that in these recently established Christian schools, application of the principle 'in loco parentis' usually includes the possibility of corporal punishment. David Pott wrote: 'At Trinity School (Tameside) three debits for irresponsible behaviour means a wallop . . .'.[32]

In analysing the concept 'in loco parentis' it is important to consider whether any biblical material is relevant and to explore how the notion of teachers being 'in loco parentis' operates in practice. There is no biblical material that makes use of the concept obligatory or prohibits it (so long as nobody claims it involves parents in entirely giving up their responsibilities). However, in one sense it is consistent with the teaching of the Bible, namely its teaching about God's fatherly care for his creation[33] and his justice and righteousness.[34] Parents and teachers may well feel that this quality of relationship commends itself to them.

In practice the concept has value but can become problematic. In commenting about teachers being 'in loco parentis' G. R. Barrell wrote: '. . . the courts have usually borne in mind that wise, prudent and careful parents do not have forty children.'[35] However, some teachers teach several hundred pupils per week, even five hundred or more and then the 'parent-substitute' model can begin to look inadequate. However, this is not the only way of looking at the teacher's role. The teacher is not only like a parent to the children. He is also 'a representative of law'.[36]

Whilst the concept of 'in loco parentis' is useful, it has a curious and unsatisfactory side to it, namely that rarely if ever in maintained schools do parents have the opportunity to decide which teacher(s) shall be in their place. This may even be unlikely in the smallish Christian schools, and even there parents can hardly be in a position to supervise constantly the internal organization of the school. There is presumably some loss of control in any real delegation.

The alleged influence of humanism on the maintained schools is the second assertion to analyse. It is probably true that many people in Britain are humanistic in practice, though not actual members of the British Humanist Association or the National Secular Society. Hence, one can not assess the extent or effect of humanism simply by ascertaining the membership figures of these organizations. However, four recurring themes frequently arise in humanist literature.

The first is that man is a rational being. One of man's highest faculties is his ability to reason, his rationality. Developing a rational mind is a key aim of education to many humanists. Being rational is held in very high esteem. It is thought that man can reason things out, can reason his way to truth in every sphere. It follows from this that humanists wish to criticize everything rationally and reject whatever cannot be shown to be true by man's rational processes. Because of this humanism tends to reject the supernatural. There is no completely adequate empirical evidence or logical argument for the existence of God or life after death (for example) so humanists either assert that pursuing answers to such questions is unprofitable, or such religious assertions are really only moral assertions[37] or they go as far as to say there is no God, there is no life after death etc. One woman, in describing how she became a humanist, wrote: 'In the end reason took over.'[38]

A second recurring theme in humanist literature is that man is on his own. Humanism is generally atheistic. Man is at the centre of the universe, not God. Man is thought to be and have the key to everything. Barbara Smoker begins her leaflet *What's This Humanism?* by claiming: 'This life, says the Humanist, is all we have . . .'.[39] In another leaflet *The World and you — a Humanist Perspective* is the statement, 'Humanists believe in people. They do not look for guidance to supernatural sources but to our human warmth, intelligence, creativity and concern.'[40] This means that in religious education, religions may be regarded as fascinating, but from a humanist perspective the reality of any supernatural realm is discounted or denied and cannot be a reliable part of acceptable answers to ultimate questions.

A third key theme in humanism is that man is sufficient. Man is developing, answering more and more questions, achieving more and more improvement. Humanist man rates himself and his abilities very highly. Man can shape his own future. A humanist has great faith in man's ability to do good to others, to live an upright life by his own effort. It is optimistic. Perhaps this is most clearly seen in the evolutionary account of man, which says, through biological, social, and psychological evolution, man is getting better. At times the problems seem great — war, crime, violence, racism, pollution, Aids, etc. — and there may be occasional bouts of pessimism, but by and large humanism is optimistic and asserts the sufficiency of man. None of the problems is insurmountable — they can all be overcome by man in time.

A fourth significant theme in humanism is 'openness'. Humanists encourage an increasingly open society — open to change and to pluralism. This view can be seen in the writings of Basil Bernstein, H.J. Blackham and James Hemming.[41] Traditional values and beliefs, traditional authority structures, are questioned and even discounted. Innovation and change are favoured. This has had an effect on education, for example, in the stance of the 'neutral chairman' encouraged by the Humanities Curriculum Project.[42] Education is not seen as an instrument for socialization, inducting pupils into the long-standing values and norms of British society, but as attempting to ensure that pupils become open to the possibility of rejecting some traditional values.

The process of analysing these humanist themes, involves identifying from a Christian perspective positive aspects, particularly in relation to education, and also aspects which may be regarded as regrettable particularly by Christians. One positive influence of humanism on education has been the general emphasis on rationality which has meant a stress on the need to have valid

reasons for what is done in education. It is not sufficient
to say, for example, 'It is the tradition in Britain' or, 'It is
what we like doing', because those are not valid reasons
in themselves. This has sometimes meant recognition of
the need to give children reasons for decisions made that
affect them and for behaviour expected of them.

A second positive influence of humanism is that there
has been a stress on general moral values, that is ones that
ought to be accepted by all people, including those who
have no belief in the reality of a supernatural realm. R.S.
Peters mentions five: commitment to the principle of
fairness and impartiality; adherence to the principle of
truth telling; acceptance that people shall in general be
free to act as they determine; recognition of the interests
of others and considering that they are as significant for
them as one's own are for oneself, and respect for
persons.[43] Similar values are given in the book *Individual
Morality* by James Hemming.[44] Peters says these are
higher order principles and they are self-evident. That is,
one cannot provide further reasons for accepting them,
but if one pursues consistently the matter of having
reasons for actions, one is always driven back to these
principles. It may be true that these principles are advocated because of a residue of Christian influence, but in
any case, they seem to be upheld by humanists and that
ought to be welcomed by Christians.

A third positive influence of humanism has sometimes
been support for the less able and underprivileged,
because of the view that every individual matters and
deserves respect. This perhaps relates to the comprehensive ideal or the principle that each pupil should have an
equal opportunity to receive an education appropriate for
them.

Fourthly, the trend towards openness (in so far as it is
genuine and not the imposition of a non-Christian view
of things) has its benefits. Schools which are trying to be
'open' are presumably not as closed to parental interest
and involvement as some schools have been in the past.
Also, such schools are presumably not closed to the ideas
and interests of pupils and hopefully are not closed to the

changing circumstances in society and therefore this might help to develop a more relevant curriculum than has sometimes been the case.

From a Christian point of view, there have also been negative influences of humanism on education. Firstly, the teacher's authority can be undermined, especially when humanism is mixed with relativism or existentialism. If pupils are taught to question everything, this can go too far, for example if they then repeatedly demand reasons for everything that is expected of them. Probably the emphasis on rationality is not intended to have this result, but there is a risk that some pupils will think it entitles them to hold up any classroom activity they wish by a demand that the teacher justify his or her request to the satisfaction of the pupils.

A second negative influence of humanism on education is the denial by humanists of the reality of the supernatural realm. In religious education, this may leave religions as fascinating areas of study, but questions of truth are likely to be avoided or at least regarded as very secondary. In denying the reality of the supernatural realm, humanism denies the truth of Christianity in so far as Christianity includes among its tenets some that involve supernatural realities. As humanism puts man at the centre of everything, and removes God from this position, increased acceptance of a humanist position is bound to be regarded by Christians (and some other religious believers) as a retrogade tendency.

Thirdly, one consequence of the denial of the existence of God, is inevitably that the notion of responsibility to God is redundant. That for Christians is bound to be seen as having regrettable implications for moral education. Openness is relevant here too, because it can easily lead to relativism, a denial of the assertion that some moral principles are 'given' and apply in every generation. Linked with this is criticism of the notion of punishment being deserved. From the acknowledgement of responsibility comes the validity of answerability and therefore of blame and punishment. It is when the notion of answerability is denied that punishment is held to be inappriorate. Instead of punishment deserved, one sometimes finds humanist preference for remedial treatment, as if all bad behaviour is only an illness. C.S. Lewis wrote about the humanitarian theory of punishment, asserting that in failing to hold man responsible for his actions (whilst instead excusing him because of heredity or upbringing) humanism reduced the value of the human person rather than defended or enhanced it.[45]

A fourth criticism of humanism is that it often appears too optimistic. In believing that man can on his own solve all the problems he is faced with, little or no account is taken of man's fallenness, which for Christians is always to be regarded as a factor limiting both adult and child capacity for good. The final chapter of this book explores a little further the implications for education of human fallenness.

Fifthly, man's rational capacities are highly regarded in the humanist view of things. From a Christian perspective they are elevated too much in humanism, because man's fallenness means his rational capacities are flawed as are his other capacities, and because knowledge of God is regarded as possible but not through rational argument alone, though there is an important place for it.

It is in the light of this kind of analysis, that some Christians favour independent Christian schools, partly because of a deep unease with what the maintained system offers and partly because of a deep conviction that it is an implication of a biblical imperative giving parents weighty obligations and responsibilities with regard to their children's upbringing and overall welfare.

Charles Martin is one writer who believes the recent Christian schools trend cannot be 'more than an interesting experiment in Britain'.[46] He also criticizes it as only a partial and inadequate response:

First, the logic of their position is that they have nothing to say to the system except to denounce it. They have no reason to argue for its improvement. They should not join in the debates about RE, assembly, discipline, sex education, comprehensive or selective. If they opt out of the system, they opt out of the debate. Secondly, they do not solve the nation's problem. If five, ten or twenty per cent

go away from the system, they won't make the problem of
the system go away. They may make things worse for the
system.[47]

Martin's point may have been valid in the early 1980s
when the Christian schools movement was rather introverted and felt little responsibility for the condition of the
maintained schools. More recently there has been a wide-
ning interest and a new awareness of reasons for seeking
improvements in the maintained system.

It was interesting to note that at the Christian Schools
conference in Bristol in March 1987 were about fifty
maintained school teachers. Some of these may have been
seeking opportunities to leave their difficult posts in
maintained schools for what they perceive as easier positions in Christian schools. However, it appears that concern for the welfare of the maintained schools is now seen
as an important Christian response even by those
involved in these Christian schools. They see Christian
schools as giving 'light' to the world (demonstrating a
valid and viable alternative model) and Christian teachers
in the maintained system as providing 'salt'.

In the Christian schools literature, both aspects are
sometimes acknowledged. At the 1984 conference one
speaker (Alan Vincent) spoke of a 'pincer movement' to
combat humanism. He 'did not see that Christian schools
spelt the end of Christian involvement in secular education. Indeed the reverse is true.'[48] A new organization
'Christians in Education', formed in January 1986 aims to
foster Christian involvement in both the maintained sector
and in Christian schools. Their leaders have experience in
both spheres.[49]

Some criticisms of Christian schools have not been
acknowledged here and ought to be mentioned, even
though they may strenuously be denied by those who
support Christian schools. It is sometimes alleged that
they are elitist and divisive. Some assert that they restrict
children too much. By educating them in an artificial 'hot-
house' environment they fail to equip children for life in
the world. Some allege that they are indoctrinatory. Alan
Storkey says they 'could be another failure to positively

respond to the integrity of the Christian faith in education. Christian schools could be a cultural retreat.'[50]

One criticism worth mentioning in the context of this book is that those involved in Christian schools are sometimes unclear about the stance and content of courses they provide in their schools. This question is not so much about the ethos or pastoral care in such schools, but more about the curriculum provided, and the direction and content of lessons. Some have found that it is much easier to start a Christian school than to be clear about what is a Christian view of each subject and how to communicate it to pupils. This has become evident when published materials from a Christian perspective seem not to be available and resources usually used in maintained schools are used also in the new Christian schools though they nowhere profess to clarify or communicate a Christian perspective. As the new style Christian schools are still in their infancy it is to be expected that a number of years are needed to consider these matters.

CHAPTER 6

Christian Education in the Church Context

This chapter considers the nature of the Christian Education which the mainstream churches provide, mainly through activities on church premises.

Over the last two hundred years most churches in Britain have invested a lot of resources in the teaching of children and young people. The Sunday Schools Movement has been part of this emphasis. Robert Raikes (1735–1811) formed a Sunday School in Gloucester in 1780 mainly for teaching children to read and to learn a catechism. He was not the originator of Sunday Schools[1] though he was the major promoter of Sunday Schools in England.

Some organizations have used the term 'Christian Education' to refer at least partly to this Sunday School work. One example is in *Experience and Faith — A Christian Education Syllabus with Parallel Themes for all-age Groups in the Church*. The title itself is some indication through its application to the Christian Education of children and adults in the churches but the Introduction begins with a more explicit statement:

For fifty years the British Lessons Council has been responsible for the preparation of outlines upon which many of the Free Churches have based their lessons for children's departments. In that time it has pioneered much that has now come to be regarded as commonplace in Christian education.[2]

This book maintains that Christian Education is much more than the instruction received. For example, it makes the following comments about a further component in Christian Education:

> It is now generally recognised that participation in the worship and fellowship of the Church is a fundamental factor in Christian education. When children come to know the Church through this kind of experience, they are most likely to grow into a true understanding of the beliefs by which the Church lives.[3]

The importance of worship, albeit in different contexts, was evident in the earlier consideration of church schools[4] and independent schools.[5]

The same publication explains why it includes in its syllabus themes for adult groups:

> The suggestions which follow should, therefore, complete an 'all-through' and 'parallel' programme of Christian education for the whole Church family. Such a programme will enable family worship in church or home to be centred around themes that all will, in one way or another, be considering. It should be helpful to parents to be studying, at a deeper level, the same themes as their children.[6]

The role of parents in relation to the various understandings of Christian Education has been mentioned before[7] but here in the context of the family and the church parents and children are involved together in the process of Christian Education much more than is possible in most schools. For Roman Catholics the role of parents and church schools has been particularly emphasized because there has been less reliance on Sunday Schools for the provision of Christian Education.

Part of the church's ministry to young people is evident from the numerous Christian youth organizations formed during the nineteenth and twentieth centuries. The following list indicates some of these and their date of foundation: National Christian Education Council 1803; YMCA 1844; YWCA 1855; Boys' Brigade 1883; Student Christian Movement 1889; Girls' Brigade 1893; Crusaders 1906; National Young Life Campaign 1913; Girl Crusaders' Union 1915; Campaigners 1922; Universities and Colleges Christian Fellowship 1928; Covenanters 1930; Church Youth Fellowships Association 1931; Methodist Association of Youth Clubs 1945; British Youth For Christ 1947; Inter-School Christian Fellowship 1947; Pathfinders 1953; Catholic Youth Service Council 1962. These have of course to some extent had their varying emphases and have developed their varying traditions but in general terms evangelism and training in discipleship have been among the main aims of such organizations. Some of these organizations have not worked within a particular church, preferring to be inter-denominational or non-denominational, but nevertheless they have influenced a considerable number of young people and must be regarded as having had a part in the Christian Education of young people.

The wisdom of supporting this concentration on work with children and young people for over two centuries is questioned by some writers[8] mainly on the clear evidence that it has not led to an increase in adult participation in church life. One writer who thinks Sunday Schools have failed wrote: 'Hundreds of thousands' of mainly working class children have attended Sunday schools but they mostly 'belonged later in life to no church'.[9]

Hull says: 'The age of eight is the high water mark of religiosity in the life cycle of many a modern person. Scepticism, secularism, rebellion, boredom, sex and pop songs set in very quickly after that pious age.'[10] The failure of most children to turn childhood participation in Sunday school into adolescent and adult participation in church life is sometimes attributed to the absence of Christian practice in their homes.[11] Recognizing what Sunday schools have not achieved does not mean denying what they did achieve in terms of providing opportunities for learning to read and for moral and religious instruction that many eighteenth and nineteenth century children did not have elsewhere.

Joslin says: 'For the most part of the current century Sunday Schools have been in decline.'[12] Where previously most Sunday schools had a few pupils who went on to become Sunday school teachers, apparently many Sunday schools are now so small that this does not happen.[13] Joslin's view is that Sunday schools have tended to become introverted, working mainly with children of those already involved with the church. He advocates increased attention to the evangelization and teaching of adults. The document referred to earlier in this chapter[14] demonstrated that some churches have for several years been giving attention to the education of adults in the church. One of Joslin's recommendations, on the basis of his experience, is that house groups can help fulfil the role of the churches.

With those who attend church fairly regularly the features of the Christian Education they receive there are evident: participation in worship[15]; a means of instruction (eg the sermon); Christian observance in the home and family,[16] and presumably a varying degree of mutual learning and encouragement through a range of informal contacts possible in the fellowship of a local church community. The place of worship, the influence of a Christian home and the effects of personal relationships in the church, perhaps indicate that Christian Education in the churches needs to be more than instruction about Christianity. For example, there must be an effect on the will, a challenge to repentance, commitment and service, and a mutual encouragement to continue in faith. The intention is not just to inform but to influence the whole person.

Joslin's concern is partly for those who do not attend activities on the church premises. In his view home groups (eg for Bible study and discussion) can have several advantages. For example, people unaccustomed to attending church can join in activities in a neighbour's home without first having to overcome the barriers associated with attending a church service with which they are unfamiliar. Also, a sense of belonging and acceptance can be built up in fairly small house groups more easily than in church services, and comments and questions from everyone present are also easier.[17] This approach fits well with Joslin's view that a life of mature discipleship is more likely to follow if there has been considerable 'instruction' before 'persuasion': 'Spiritual problems arise where inadequate instruction has been too hastily followed by impatient persuasion.'[18]

The insights of Joslin may be helpful, but concentration on the teaching of adults, through house meetings or by any other means, can be no panacea. The churches need to give continuing thought to their work with children and young people. To neglect this whilst being submerged in adult work would not be helpful. In the church context Christian Education quite properly embraces both children and adults. There should be no emphasis on either at the expense of the other. The growth of the 'Family Service' has been one attempt to involve families together in worship and learning and thereby balance the frequent division of congregations into departments selected according to age.[19]

The effectiveness of Christian Education in the church context should not be judged only or even mainly by the numerical stength of the congregations. That is to view Christian Education in pragmatic or functional terms alone. Sometimes the main motive for concentration on work with children appears to have been the future health of the churches. This kind of thinking is perhaps typified by the title of the book, 'Today's Children, Tomorrow's Church'.[20]

There are deficiencies in thinking that priorities for Christian Education in the churches can be ascertained by identifying the age group which has most potential in terms of numbers likely to be loyal members in forthcoming years. One is that it is impossible to tell with any certainty which group has the most potential. Another is the false assumption that strength will be in one particular age group. Another is that it is inconsistent with Christian theology to think that one group matters more than another. People matter because they are human beings[21] not because they can make the greatest contribution to the church of the future.

The concept of 'continuing' or 'lifelong' education

which has gained credence in recent years, may point to something valuable for the church. There seems to be little awareness of the relevance of Christian Education for old people, presumably because the purpose of Christian Education has tended to be to strengthen the church of the future and old people are regarded as having little to contribute to this. With the trend towards earlier retirement and greater life expectancy, those aged over fifty may be more significant than ever before. It is not that here is another group which might have exclusive attention, but that a healthy view of Christian Education in the church context embraces everyone within it regardless of age. This includes recognition that quality matters as well as quantity and that future usefulness to the church is not the most important criterion in assessing quality.

One aspect of this matter of quality is the degree to which the Christian Education helps church people to relate their faith to their contemporary situation. John Hull makes it abundantly clear in his book *What Prevents Christian Adults from Learning?*[22] that features of modernity affect the context and role of Christian Education. Whilst his main concern in this book is with the Christian Education of adults in the churches, the same must be true of the Christian Education of children and young people in the churches.

He refers to one feature as 'objective pluralization'.[23] Part of this plurality is the variety of Christian denominations that exist. Another aspect of it is the close presence of other religions. Yet another aspect is the inner fragmentation that can arise when one person has several different roles. For example, one person may be employee, child, parent, churchgoer, sports club member and so on. To some extent a range of beliefs and values is offered within and between these situations. John Hull's strong conviction is that Christian Education must be much more than transmission.[24] It must explore and clarify the situations in which Christians live. It must help Christians relate their faith to the apparently competing belief stances and world views they meet. If it does not, then it increases the likelihood of the Christian's faith being an isolated, compartmentalized matter, unrelated to the real world. Providing opportunities for understanding the various value options and religions available has thus become essential, even if traditionally such opportunities have not been included in the activities of some churches.

One might have thought that Christian Education in the churches would be confined exclusively to education in Christianity. Perhaps that has been the case in many churches. Christians of all ages need something broader than this for at least the same reasons as those given in chapter 2 to support the case that pupils need a religious education broader than Christianity alone.[25] If Christian Education within the churches is to be broad enough to include the various value options and religions available, this has implications for the training of ministers, lay preachers, Sunday school teachers and youth leaders. It is likely that many of these people themselves need opportunities to explore the various value options and religions being offered for acceptance in contemporary British society.

CHAPTER 7

Christian Education under Review

The previous chapters do not exhaust the variety of ways in which the expression 'Christian Education' is used. For example, in a review of a book on the Bible[1] Peter Woodward says, 'Too much Christian education consists of telling children about the Bible in a way which diverts them from coming directly to it, as they are able.'[2] The precise application of the phrase 'Christian Education' is not made clear but since the reviewer commends the book to 'everybody involved in church education, all Christian educators, and most teachers of Religious Education'[3] he presumably has in mind an application at least that wide. The term has also been used to refer to a partnership in Christian Education in which both Day and Sunday schools are deemed to be participating.[4] The expression can also function as shorthand for 'education about Christianity', perhaps referring to the exploration of Christianity in a multifaith course.

There may of course be still other usages. However, those explored in chapters 2 — 6 are enough to illustrate that because the phrase is used in a variety of ways, there can be effective communication when it is used only if there is vigilance in clarifying the meaning in mind. It is not that there is wide agreement on its meaning which can be taken for granted and that the variety of usages is merely in the differing contexts where it applies. Familiarity with its currency in one context may tend to obscure the different understanding of it which others can have.

It is true that the varying references to Christian Education sometimes employ the same terminology in their descriptions of it. For example, several understandings of Christian Education refer to the place of worship in Christian Education[5] but that does not mean that their understanding of Christian Education is altogether the same. One reason for asserting this is that their understanding of worship may be somewhat different. The charismatic worship of some recently established Christian schools can be much more informal and spontaneous than the liturgical worship in some churches and some independent schools with a Christian foundation. Another reason is that some understandings of Christian Education give a high priority to an aspect scarcely present in another understanding of it. For example, in Christian Education in the churches the role of parents is often a crucial and integral aspect, but in independent boarding schools it does not have such a vital place for many of the pupils.

It might be argued that the aims of Christian Education in the varying contexts are the same and the different contexts merely reflect different means to this same end, or that the differences in the varying contexts are only a matter of degree. There may be some truth in both of these assertions, but when the different understandings of Christian Education are compared it appears that their understanding of the aims of Christian Education is not altogether the same. These differences in aims partly reflect different theological emphases. One Christian tradition puts a high priority on individual conversion and faith. Other traditions put a high priority on sacramental worship or on service to the community or on denominational loyalty. This is to be expected when one considers that the term 'Christian Education' is used by Anglicans, Roman Catholics, members of the mainstream Free Churches and by recently established independent churches and fellowships. Their theology and practice, including their understanding of what being a Christian means, varies to some extent and is therefore likely to affect their understanding of Christian Education.

Some earlier chapters[6] have indicated that the credibility of the notion of Christian Education has been questioned, notably by Paul Hirst. Whatever the differences or common ground between the variety of usages of the phrase 'Christian Education', they are all suspect if the criticism that the whole idea of a Christian Education is 'a kind of nonsense'[7] is justified. This being so, it is important to understand and analyse Paul Hirst's view of the concept and this chapter now concentrates on this task.

In his 1971 article[8] Hirst said that whereas at one time subjects like maths, engineering and farming were at least partly understood by reference to one's religious beliefs, now these have an autonomy, where right and wrong is determined by rational principles. Also, he asserts, education has a similarly autonomous status.

Hirst anticipated that Christians would respond by saying that since Christians and humanists disagree on some points, there must be a distinctively Christian concept of education, namely that a Christian 'will want his children brought up in the Christian faith'.[9] This he calls a 'primitive' concept of education. He prefers a 'sophisticated' view of education, in which it is 'concerned with passing on beliefs and practices according to, and together with, their objective status'.[10] In this view there are canons of objectivity and reason against which Christian beliefs must be assessed.

In response to Hirst's position, several points can be made. In his 1965 paper, 'Liberal Education and the Nature of Knowledge'[11] Hirst listed seven distinct disciplines or forms of knowledge. In his 1973 paper, 'The forms of Knowledge Re-visited'[12] he said: 'It was no part of the thesis even in its earliest foundation that the forms of knowledge are totally independent of each other, sharing no concepts or logical rules. That the forms are interrelated has been stressed from the start.'[13] Hirst has maintained that the forms of knowledge are autonomous or logically distinct[14] — this means they are in his view distinct from each other. It should be noted that religion appears in the 1965 list of forms[15] and was still there when the article was reprinted in 1974[16], though in a 1973 article[17] he said he did not know if it was a form of knowledge. This original confidence and later hesitation suggests that at least at some points Hirst's scheme is not altogether firm and clear.

Whilst we may well be able to distinguish several forms of knowledge, they are inter-related and have to be, in the process of forming a coherent view of the world as a whole. Peters has argued[18] that an educated man is not just knowledgeable in his field, but is someone who relates his field to others, forming a coherent pattern of life. From this perspective it is legitimate to relate one discipline or form (eg religion) to another (eg education). It might be objected that education is not a form of knowledge but against this is the position in Hirst's 1971 article[19] where mathematics, engineering, farming and, by implication, education are all referred to as 'pursuits'. It is in the task of relating a religion (eg Christianity) to education that a religious (or Christian) view of education emerges and does so even if education is a pursuit rather than a form of knowledge. It appears that Hirst wants one area, namely logical rules, to influence all other forms of knowledge, but denies that religion should or sensibly could have a similar role.

A comprehensive understanding of many contemporary issues (eg Aids, conservation, disarmament, pollution, world population growth) is not possible if a particular pursuit or form is entirely autonomous. To understand these problems one has to draw on various disciplines and it is sometimes possible to bring the concepts and evidence of one discipline or form to bear on a matter which also comes within the ambit of another discipline or form and to do so without a nonsensical relating of concepts.

At two points Hirst seems to oversimplify a matter. Firstly, he wrongly assumes that the only response of Christians will be to want their children brought up in the Christian faith whereas Christians often have a far broader interest in education than this[20] and by no means always prefer for their children an indoctrination that conditions them to respond in a narrow and prescribed way. Secondly, he commends objectivity without acknowledging how notoriously difficult it is to have complete objectivity, since every thinker and reseacher brings much that is subjective to his work.

Christians may well have theological reasons for objecting to Hirst's rejection of the notion of Christian Education. These arise because Christian theology is a comprehensive structure of doctrines which have implications in many areas of life, including education. This can be demonstrated in various ways. For example, on one hand there is good theological reason to maintain that some genuine knowledge is possible for everyone regardless of religious belief or experience. Christian beliefs about common grace, general revelation, and the continuing though spoilt image of God in man, support this view. To maintain that some knowledge is possible regardless of religious belief and experience is important for education. However, on the other hand the concept of special revelation can contribute to education an aspect that is not there if education is confined to the rational development of autonomous persons. If one believes that particular revelation or illumination is possible that also is significant in one's view of education. This possibility of relating both general and special revelation to education, constitutes one reason for asserting that Christian theology can be related to education.

Another theological point arises from Hirst's high confidence in the rational capacities of human beings. He appears to give little or no place to the Christian notion of human fallenness. This concept arose in a different context in an earlier chapter and is relevant again in the next and final chapter.[21] Since the Reformation it has been widely accepted in Christianity that the fall has affected every area of human personality. If belief in the fallenness of humanity is accepted, there is at least a question about the constant reliability of the rational capacities. Many Christians would go further and assert that their understanding of the doctrine of the fall definitely rejects the view that reason remains unaffected. Hirst's position seems to rely heavily on the reliability of human rationality.

One further area of Christian theology that is relevant is the belief in God's sovereignty and omniscience. This includes a belief that God has complete knowledge about the whole universe. Paul acknowledged human dependence on God when at Athens he quoted a Greek poet who said, 'In him we live and move and have our being.'[22] From Paul's statement that 'in him (Christ) all things hold together',[23] it can be inferred that we do not live in a world containing several 'autonomous' disciplines or forms of thought, but rather in a universe which is one entity kept together by Christ. One consequence of such a belief is that never will a relating of (true) knowledge in one area to (true) knowledge in another area result in a contradiction. If there is an apparent contradiction, the apparent knowledge is at some point or points partial or not actual knowledge, or knowledge in one area is not correctly understood in relation to knowledge in another area. This belief in the unity of the world need not lead to a non-sensical relating of concepts such as talking about 'magnetic fields being angry'.[24] Maintaining that aspects of knowledge cannot be contradictory, does not imply that all concepts can be related in a direct and meaningful way.

Hirst expanded his views on this topic in a lecture in 1978[25] and in it the idea of a Christian concept of education was treated with less hostility. It is not seen as 'a kind of nonsense' or a 'huge mistake' as it was in 1971[26], though it is still regarded as a 'primitive' and 'inadequate' concept of education.

Hirst calls this 'primitive' concept of education 'catechesis', and his 'sophisticated' concept of education 'education in natural reason'[27] and says that 'education and catechesis, based respectively in reason and faith, are properly to be seen as complementary'.[28] Also, he regards the outcomes aimed at by 'open-ended religious education' and by 'committed religious catechesis', as 'perfectly compatible'.[29] Further, he speaks of the relationship between faith and reason as one in which faith is 'a complement to reason'.[30]

In applying this distinction to church schools Hirst says he can 'see only one way out for the Church School . . . and that is if the activities of education and catechesis are sharply separated within the school, being self-consciously and deliberately presented to the pupils as clearly different in character and objectives.'[31] He goes on to say that 'whereas education will be dominated by a concern for the justificatory status of beliefs by natural reasoning, and demand response solely on that basis, catechesis will present beliefs so as to challenge pupils to free response.'[32] As Hirst presented this lecture to a Roman Catholic audience it may be no surprise that the treatment of a Christian perspective on education is somewhat more sympathetic here, but his position needs to be analysed carefully.

In this further analysis the first point to note is that Hirst's use of the terms 'primitive' and 'sophisticated' is unhelpful because they are not neutral, purely descriptive terms. 'Primitive' has in common usage pejorative overtones and 'sophisticated' can imply 'superior'. In view of this, care should be taken to ensure that these terms do not influence judgment more than is warranted. Hirst may not have satisfactorily demonstrated that using these terms in this way is justified on rational grounds. For example, if parents (or a society) were to be convinced that particular beliefs are true and valuable and *not* want their children (or the next generation) to accept these beliefs, that could well be considered to be irrational. If parents are convinced of the truth and value of particular beliefs it is reasonable that they should want others to accept them. To reduce the risk of scoring a point by the somewhat hidden implications of the terms 'primitive' and 'sophisticated' one could speak of the first and second concepts of education which Hirst described.

Early in this lecture Hirst appears to recognize two concepts of education but regarding them both as kinds of education is not maintained. This inconsistency is a further criticism of Hirst's position. He inserts 'catechesis' for the 'primitive' kind of education, and reference to 'education in natural reason' gives way to references simply to 'education'. This has the effect of 'cornering the market', trying to monopolize use of the term 'education', trying to reserve the use of the term to mean what he does and to deny its legitimate use in other ways. He replaces the first concept of education with an alternative term (catechesis) but does not do so with the second concept of education. To be consistent and to avoid the impression that the first concept of education does not warrant being regarded as education, an alternative expression should be coined for the second concept of education also. Perhaps 'rational training' would be appropriate or 'reduction training' since the intention is to reduce everything to questions of 'objectivity and reason'.[33]

This criticism of Hirst's position can be extended by a closer examination of the way he contrasts education and catechesis. Insufficient justification is given for this contrast. He fails to demonstrate that education can only mean a process in which natural reasoning dominates. 'Education in natural reason'[34] is a very limited and limiting concept of education. It is not clear that areas of the curriculum such as art, craft, music, drama, literature, careers education, physical education and religious education will be adequately conceived if 'On this second view, the character of education is in the end determined simply by the canons of objectivity and reason appropriate to the different forms of knowledge and understanding that we have.'[35] What qualifies as knowledge in these areas is one crucial aspect, but there is much more to each area than a rational analysis of truth claims. For example, great works of art cannot be reduced to statements amenable to verification according to particular truth criteria, without overlooking much that is involved in their being great works of art. Also, there is much more to religion and religious education than the doctrinal aspects or truth claims which can be identified and assessed 'by the canons of objectivity and reason'.[36]

Sometimes Hirst has supported a concept of education somewhat less narrow than that in this 1978 lecture. For example, in his article, 'Liberal education and the nature of knowledge'[37] he said, 'Certainly liberal education as is here being understood is only one part of the education a person ought to have, for it omits quite deliberately for instance specialist education, physical education and character training.'[38] However, what Hirst describes in this 1978 lecture as 'education in natural reason' or 'education' seems to be the same as the 'liberal education' he earlier regarded as a limited or restricted kind of education.[39]

This argument can be taken further because concentration on education in natural reason may not accord with some views of the nature and responses of children. In

Christian theology, though different aspects of human nature can be identified, such as body and mind-soul-spirit, these cannot be separated out but operate in a 'psycho-somatic unity'. In this sense the nature of every child is such that they cannot respond at an exclusively intellectual level. Education which concentrates on the development of mind more than or at the expense of development in other areas is a biassed kind of education in a way that education concerned with the development of the whole child is not. If education concentrates too much on mental development, this implies that emotional or spiritual or physical development is less important.

Also, as a matter of practical possibility, teachers cannot ensure that children concern themselves in any task only with questions of objectivity and reason. They respond as whole people. In the case of Christianity no teacher can guarantee that children will feel the challenge of it (or aspects of it) only in the catechesis context, whereas Hirst appears to want to confine personal challenge to that context.

Another point to question is Hirst's view of the stance of the county schools regarding religion. He rightly says that 'our totally state financed schools are not officially at present religiously uncommitted'[40] and then goes on to imply that they would be religiously uncommitted if they concentrated on 'education in the particular sense I have outlined'[41] and omitted, for example, school worship which is 'catechetical rather than educational'.[42] However, to exclude worship would be to take up a stance towards religion and to say something about religion, namely that collective worship is considered to entail elements which make its provision in state financed schools undesirable on rational grounds. Schools would then be committed to a different stance on religion but not to no position at all.

Hirst said that 'the schools of our religiously pluralist society are . . . moving steadily to a secular position as a result of social forces'.[43] Whilst this may be true of some schools, it is not true of all, perhaps particularly not true of most church schools, and it is in any case not a reason why Christians should in principle welcome or prefer this claimed 'secular position' of society at large or prefer schools to exchange a hitherto religiously committed position for a secular one.

In his consideration of Christian Education Hirst seems to have in mind school situations rather than church situations where, as chapter 6 showed, the concept is still used. This chapter has indicated that the meaning of Christian Education is to some extent dependent upon what is meant by the terms 'Christian' and 'education'.[44] Chapters 2 – 6 considered five contexts in which the terms 'Christian' and 'education' are used together, the word 'Christian' functioning to distinguish a particular type of education. Though with varying emphases in meaning and method, Christian Education in all these contexts seeks to foster Christian faith and discipleship as these are understood in each particular context.

It is noteworthy that four of these usages (those considered in chapters 3–6) altogether avoid the largest area of educational enterprise, namely the county schools, and the fifth (considered in chapter 2) related only to religious education in county schools, not with the major part of the curriculum. This prompts the question whether Christianity can still have implications for education in county schools or whether the nature of British society is now so secular or so plural that implications from Christianity should not be sought because so few people have any degree of acceptance of Christianity itself. The extent of secularization in Britain has been considered earlier[45] and the case for regarding Britain as somewhat but not altogether secular will not be repeated here.

The next chapter explores the possible implications of Christianity for the county schools in the contemporary situation. Expressed like this it could appear that the education in county schools is accepted in an a priori fashion as being other than Christian and so no amount of implications from Christianity could render it Christian Education. Whether at least in the county school context it would be more accurate to speak of 'a Christian view of education' or 'a Christian contribution to education' rather than of 'Christian Education' is a question which will be left until the next chapter.[46]

CHAPTER 8

Relating the Concept Christian Education
to County Schools

It is quite reasonable for the term 'Christian Education' to
be used with reference to the education provided in
schools with some kind of church or Christian foundation
and in the church context itself. However, this leaves out
the question of whether Christian theology has anything
to say about the education of those who come from no
Christian background and make no Christian profession
or about the education available in schools with no church
or Christian foundation, particularly the county schools.
It is the contention of this chapter that at the present time
Christian theology has much to contribute to education in
county schools. The assertion is that this contribution is
still valid in a multifaith society and that it should not be
neglected through an exclusive concentration on Christian
Education as it applies within the Christian community.

The church school experience suggests that this wider
contribution of Christian perspectives might be welcomed.
An earlier chapter noted that some church schools continue to be popular, even to the point of being over sub-
scribed.[1] This preference for what church schools have to
offer comes sometimes from parents practising a religion
other than Christianity and sometimes from those with no
particular religious affiliation. This raises at least the
possibility that Christianity is having some implications

for these church schools which non-Christian parents find acceptable and even desirable. The wider question is then whether Christianity should have implications for the county schools and whether there would be support for such implications in the present multifaith context of British society.

In some parts of England Christianity continues to have an influence on the education in county schools through the headteachers and staff appointed. One piece of recent research showed that in Gloucestershire over four-fifths of the headteachers of county primary schools claim affiliation to one of the Christian denominations.[2] That personal practice confirms the validity of the claims made by these headteachers is seen in the finding that of all the primary school heads in Gloucestershire, 'Two in every five (42%) attend church most weeks and a further 14% attend regularly at least once a month.'[3]

The religious views of these headteachers appeared to be having some bearing on the kind of assemblies usually held in their schools. The research showed that in 71% of the county schools assemblies were regarded as Christian in one sense or another. 'For 41% of the county schools the major emphasis of assemblies is described as implicitly Christian, while for 28% the major emphasis is described as explicitly Christian but not denominational. Just 2% of the county schools claim that the major emphasis of their assemblies is explicitly Christian and denominational.'[4]

In considering the findings regarding religious education (excluding the assemblies) it must be remembered that the Gloucestershire Agreed Syllabus states that the content of religious education 'will be drawn largely from the study of Christianity in its many forms . . .'.[5] The research report states: 'While very few (2%) claim to ignore the agreed syllabus altogether, only 3% claim to follow it very closely. Of the other 95%, one-third follow it quite closely, while two-thirds follow it only in general terms.'[6]

Leslie Francis summarizes his findings concerning Gloucestershire county schools as follows: '. . . Christianity is still far from dead in county schools in Gloucestershire. The data present a much more traditionally

Christian picture than current educational theory seems to provide.'[7] and, 'Many county schools promote a Christian presence in education and foster contact with the churches.'.[8]

Francis contends that it is not unreasonable to regard Gloucestershire as representative of the shire counties in general.[9] Even if he is correct, the possible implications of Christian beliefs for education need to be argued for on a still broader basis. It is necessary to give examples that apply more widely than in assemblies and religious education. The two examples below focus on aspects of the Christian doctrine of humanity. These are deliberately selected because education so centrally involves people.

Part of the Christian doctrine of humanity is that every human being is created by God and made in his image.[10] There is a substantial body of literature which explores the meaning of this doctrine.[11] It includes asserting that every person matters, has inherent worth, has some moral awareness and has a capacity for spiritual life.

The implications of this for education are perhaps obvious — that every child has value, simply because he or she is human. The value of pupils is not conditional upon their achievements. This involves giving every pupil an education appropriate to their age, abilities and aptitudes[12] rather than regarding each pupil as merely secondary to the needs of society. This is not to say it is acceptable to ignore the wider needs of the community, but it is to deny the validity of any utilitarian view of education that means the welfare of the individual is subordinated or the most important aim of education is preparation for the world of work. It therefore follows that over-emphasis on the development of the technological skills needed by modern society, should be avoided because it treats the pupils as means to an end rather than as having the much greater value and significance which being in the image of God confers.

Another implication of regarding every pupil as being in the image of God, is that every pupil should be helped to appreciate spiritual and moral values. This includes attention to the creative and affective areas rather than regarding education in a purely functional way in which, for example, the major aim might be to equip pupils to secure maximum material prosperity once they leave school.

Christian beliefs about human fallenness[13] are also relevant here. It is not that the image of God is denied or altogether cancelled by human fallenness[14] but it is to acknowledge that it has some damaging affect on people. Put another way, this entails recognizing that the human situation is one in which as well as there being much that is noble and wholesome, there is also a temptation towards evil and even a tendency towards it. If this is accepted as the human condition, one implication for education is that every child has a potential for good which should be promoted, and faces moral choices and temptations to evil which require the development of discernment and self-discipline.

At a somewhat broader level, there are general values and principles, which have biblical support, which are important to Christians, which significantly affect the character and ethos of schools, and which can command acceptance much more widely than in the Christian constituency alone. Commitment to honesty and truth telling are examples. Others were referred to in an earlier chapter[15]. They are relevant because education is inevitably a value laden concept. In no county school can education avoid encouraging some values. Hence it can be extremely beneficial to have values which can be supported by a large majority of parents — Christians and others.

An education which takes these values seriously and upholds the view of human dignity and the human predicament mentioned earlier[16] can be consistent with Christian beliefs and principles, and certainly not be anti-Christian or neutral as regards values. In this sense it could be described as Christian Education.

Used in this way the term 'Christian Education' does not indicate that the content of religious education is Christianity (though it may be), nor that the explicit aim is the nurturing of Christian faith (though it may have that consequence for some pupils). It does indicate that the character of the school, or more particularly the values generally upheld in it, are Christian values, albeit of a fairly elementary kind (eg about commitment to honesty and the care of individuals). These basic values are ones which Christians can wholeheartedly affirm — without any shame or embarrassment. Education built on such values can in one sense legitimately be described as Christian because Christians can endorse with integrity these basic values and this view of humanity.

The existence of Christian Education in this sense may well be not in the least inimical to the further development of a multicultural society. It could even be argued that a Christian view of humanity and justice is a fine foundation for a multicultural society. If a different view of humanity and justice were to prevail in which some people become regarded as dispensable or as inferior citizens, it could be then that the existence of several religious and cultural stances alongside each other in one society becomes vulnerable. Hence the fostering of such values is not a non-Christian or sub-Christian pursuit, but a vital Christian task.

Some Christians might respond to this by saying that the description 'Christian Education' should be allowed only where all the teaching staff of a school are Christians and all lessons indicate and commend a Christian view of the content of the lesson. However, that would be too strict a requirement and would probably involve maintaining that there never has been Christian Education in any school, since there needs to be only one lesson in which a Christian insight or perspective is overlooked or in which a non-Christian position is inadvertently propogated, for the strict standard to be missed. The possibility of interpreting Christian Education in such an extreme way illustrates the fact that whether or not any particular educational process or situation warrants the description 'Christian Education' is not a simple all or nothing matter but rather a case of degrees. Many situations are 'more' or 'less' Christian, rather than fully Christian or not at all Christian.

Some people may prefer to speak of 'a Christian perspective on education' or 'a Christian view of education', even when considering education based on the values outlined in this chapter. They might maintain that one can have 'a Christian view of education' in county schools but that the term 'Christian Education' can never be valid for the county school context, whatever values prevail. Clearly Christianity and education are not identical. However, the major danger with the phrase, 'a Christian view of education' is that it can imply a complete separation between Christianity and education, as if education is inevitably an enterprise entirely distinct from Christianity. This book maintains that since they are both concerned about values they can come together in the matter of values. The phrase, 'a Christian view of education' can appear to imply that education is a process which Christians can examine only as onlookers observing something entirely separate, whereas the process itself can be shaped by Christian values. Education is not a process that can secure itself in a world of its own, unaffected by value questions. When education is based on values that are consonant with Christianity it can then meaningfully be described as Christian Education. However, the contention that these values and a Christian view of humanity can still legitimately have a fundamental place in the life of county schools does not rest on whether this is described as Christian Education or as a Christian view of education.

In the 1960s and earlier, the relevance of Christianity for the county schools was more often enunciated, than has been the case in the 1970s and 1980s. Much of the earlier literature speaks naturally and confidently about it. The more recent multifaith nature of society, including the pupils in many schools, may have been a major influence in the tendency to assume that in the changed context Christian thought has less to contribute. This chapter does not claim that the notion of Christian Education is not important in the various contexts explored in chapters 2 — 6, but it does seek to demonstrate that at the level of values it continues to be a valid and meaningful concept when applied to county schools. This implies that further investigation into the relationship of Christianity to schools that have little or no overtly Christian foundation could be worthwhile.

Two particular questions arise from the way the term

'Christian Education' is used in this chapter. First, can relating education to the Christian doctrine of humanity and general moral values ever be the basis of education that justifies the description 'Christian Education', whilst it appears never to mention Christ who has a central place in Christianity? Second, does the Bible have only one model of the nature of man, namely as a creature who is in the image of God but also fallen, noble but flawed? In response to this second question it should be noted that the Bible has at least two other models of man. There is Christ, the Son of Man,[17] who is 'the image of the invisible God'[18] and who 'committed no sin'.[19] Also, there is redeemed man made possible, according to Christian belief, by the work of Christ.

The first question raises matters far more controversial than the beliefs about the fundamental nature of human beings. People with a wide variety of religious convictions accept general statements about all children having value quite apart from any academic achievements, about there being a non-material dimension to life and so on. However, when there are statements more specifically about Christ and redemption, there is no such broad consensus of opinion. Asserting that every child matters is more likely to be accepted in our present society than trying to include reference to beliefs about Christ and redemption in discussions about education.

In terms of moral education it might be said that children should be helped to see Christ as a person of exemplary moral character and to feel drawn to trying to live a life of similar moral rectitude. Belief in Christ as a unique person particularly in terms of the quality of his moral life could have this kind of implication for moral education. However, it could be argued that inviting children to follow the moral example of Christ is inconsistent with a belief in the fallenness of humanity unless there is also a belief that some way of overcoming the results of their fallenness is available to them all. Otherwise it is bound to be desperately depressing for children if Christ is seen only as a superior example which leaves them struggling to reach an impossibly high standard with grossly insufficient power to do so.

Belief that Christ made redemption possible has implications also for any discussion about individual potential or understanding life. Several publications refer to the aims of education in terms which leave open the question of what precisely is human potential. The Norwood Report 1943 stated that the first aim of education is 'to help each individual to realize the full powers in his personality — body, mind and spirit.'[20] A more recent publication said, 'A school's task is to equip pupils for adult life by developing all their qualities and talents.'[21] and another said, 'There is wide agreement about the purpose of learning at school, in particular that pupils should develop lively, enquiring minds, acquire understanding, knowledge and skills relevant to adult life and employment and develop personal moral values.'[22]

In response to such statements it may be asked if the qualities and understanding to be developed include redemption. This partly involves asking if 'understanding' and 'personal moral values' encompass understanding redemption and eternal destiny, and personal commitment to the value of redemption. If it were proposed that a Christian view of Christ and redemption should be inculcated in county schools, that would not be acceptable to many parents in our present plural society. There might well be widespread support for exploring the core beliefs of Christianity, but that is not the same as encouraging pupils to accept that they are true.

This perhaps indicates one reason why some Christians support separate Christian schools, whether financially independent or to some extent maintained from public funds. They believe that only in separate Christian schools is there freedom to allow the whole range of Christian beliefs to influence and permeate every area of the school's life, particularly beliefs about Christ and redemption. It is probably the case that the extent to which beliefs about Christ and redemption can in practice have implications for education in the county schools will vary from one part of the country to another, from one era to another, from one school to another and even from one part of the school curriculum to another. Though on a national scale there may not be support for making a Christian view of Christ and redemption central in the life of county schools, there might be support for this in some areas. This could be the subject of further enquiry. Uncertainty about this should not detract from the importance of maintaining that a Christian view of humanity and general moral values can legitimately be the key to the value base of county schools and that this can receive widespread support in the closing years of the twentieth century.

The Religious Provisions of the Education Act 1944

RELIGIOUS INSTRUCTION

Section 7 This gives local education authorities the duty 'to contribute towards the spiritual, moral, mental and physical development' of children. In particular they must ensure that the provisions of clauses 25 and 26 are carried out.

Section 25(2) This states that '. . . religious instruction shall be given in every county school and every voluntary school.'

Section 25(4) This gives parents the right to withdraw their children from religious instruction.

Section 26 This says that religious instruction '. . . shall be given in accordance with an agreed syllabus . . . and shall not include any catechism or formulary which is distinctive of any particular religious denomination'. This is the famous 'Cowper–Temple' clause — section 14 of the Education Act 1870, also re-enacted in section 28 of the Education Act 1921. The law officers of the Crown said that the ten commandments, the Lord's Prayer and the Apostles' Creed are not distinctive of any particular denomination.

Section 27(1) Where parents of pupils at controlled schools request that religious instruction be given in accordance with the school's trust deed (or else in accordance with practice in the school before it became a controlled school) the foundation managers/governors shall, unless they think it unreasonable, arrange for such religious instruction to be given at the school during not more than two periods in each week.

Section 28 Religious instruction at aided/special agreement schools shall be under the control of the governors and shall be in accordance with trust deeds (or else with practice previously observed in the school). If parents want religious instruction to be in accordance with any agreed syllabus adopted by the local education authority (and pupils cannot with reasonable convenience attend any school using the syllabus) then the managers/governors shall make arrangements for religious instruction in accordance with the syllabus to be given and if they are unwilling the arrangements shall be made by the authority.

Section 29 and the Fifth Schedule set down how the Agreed Syllabuses are to be drawn up.

Section 30 The position of teachers. For example, no teacher in a county or voluntary school shall be penalized because he gives religious instruction and no teacher in a county school shall be required to give religious instruction.

Section 77(2) This says that the Secretary of State shall 'cause inspections to be made of every educational establishment . . .'. However, HMIs may not inspect religious instruction of a denominational character in voluntary schools, though the appropriate governing/managing body may arrange such inspections.

Section 77(3) This says that any local education authority 'may cause an inspection to be made of any educational establishment maintained by the authority . . .'. Religious instruction is not exempt from the HMI or LEA inspections, except as mentioned in section 77(2).

Fifth Schedule. This says that if the conference set up to prepare an Agreed Syllabus cannot agree, or if the Secretary of State considers that a local education authority has failed to adopt a syllabus unanimously recommended to them by the conference, the Secretary of state may arrange for a syllabus to be prepared which shall be adopted.

RELIGIOUS WORSHIP

Section 25(1) This says that the school day in every county and voluntary school shall begin with collective worship on the part of all pupils in attendance at the school, though it is not a requirement to assemble the whole school together for this if the local education authority for county schools and the governing body for voluntary schools consider that the school premises make it impracticable to assemble all pupils together.

Section 25(4) Parents may request the withdrawal of their children from worship and then the pupils 'shall be excused'.

Section 26 This says that the worship in county schools must not 'be distinctive of any particular religious denomination'.

Section 30 No teacher may be required to attend worship or may be penalized because he attends or omits to attend worship.

The Religious Provisions of the Education Reform Act 1988

Section 1 The curriculum for maintained schools must be 'a balanced and broadly based curriculum which (a) promotes the spiritual, moral, cultural, mental and physical development of pupils at the school and of society'. RE contributes to these areas, particularly the spiritual and moral areas. The Secretary of State, local education authorities, governing bodies and head-teachers all have a duty to exercise their functions with a view to securing the kind of curriculum stated.

Section 2(1) The *basic* curriculum for every maintained school shall include (a) religious education for all registered pupils (b) the National Curriculum for all registered pupils of compulsory school age. It should be noted that the term 'religious instruction' is not now used, but 'religious education' is used instead.

Section 6(1) All pupils attending a maintained school 'shall on each school day take part in an act of collective worship' though section 9 allows parents to withdraw their children.

Section 6(2) Schools may have a single act of worship for all pupils or separate ones for pupils in different age groups.

Section 6(7) 'school group' means any group in which pupils are taught or take part in other school activities.

Section 7(1) In county schools the collective worship 'shall be wholly or mainly of a broadly Christian character.'

Section 7(2) '. . . collective worship is of a broadly Christian character if it reflects the broad traditions of Christian belief, without being distinctive of any particular denomination'.

Section 7(3) It is not necessary for every act of worship to comply with 7(1) 'provided that, taking any school term as a whole, most such acts which do take place in the school do comply . . .'

Section 7(4) and (5) The extent to which acts of worship comply or do not comply with 7(1) 'shall be such as may be appropriate having regard to 5(a) any circumstances relating to the family backgrounds of the pupils concerned which are relevant for determining the character of the collective worship which is appropriate in their case and (b) their ages and aptitudes.'

Section 8(2) RE is still to be of the kind required by sections 26–28 of the 1944 Act.

Section 8(3) Any new agreed syllabus 'shall reflect the fact that the religious traditions in Great Britain are in the main Christian whilst taking account of the teaching and practices of the other principal religions represented in Great Britain'.

Section 9 The 1944 provision (Section 25(5)) for withdrawal from RE and/or worship remains unchanged except that the new clauses refer to religious education.

Section 10 It is the duty of the local education authority, the governing body and the headteacher to secure '(a) that all pupils in attendance at the school take part in the daily collective worship required by section 6 and (b) that religious education is given in accordance with section 2(1)(a).'

Section 11(1) It is the duty of every LEA to constitute a standing advisory council on religious education to advise on school worship and RE and to carry out the functions conferred by section 12.

Section 11(2) In particular the SACRE may give advice on 'methods of teaching, the choice of materials and the provision of training for teachers.'

Section 11(3) and (4) The SACRE must consist of people appointed by the authority to represent

(a) 'such Christian and other religious denominations as, in the opinion of the authority, will appropriately reflect the principal religious traditions of the area.'

(b) the Church of England (except in Wales)

(c) 'such associations representing teachers as, in the opinion of the authority ought, having regard to the circumstances of the area, to be represented;

and (d) the authority'

If an adopted Agreed Syllabus is used at a grant-maintained school, or more than one, the governing body or bodies may appoint a person to be a member of the SACRE. SACRE may include co-opted members.

Section 11(9) The SACRE shall in each year publish a report.

Section 12(1) On application by the head teacher of a county school, it is the duty of the SACRE to consider whether it is appropriate for the requirement for Christian collective worship to apply in the case of that school, or in the case of any class or descriptions of pupils at that school.

Section 12(2) In determining whether it is appropriate for the Christian collective worship to apply, the council must have regard to any circumstances relating to the family backgrounds of the relevant pupils.

Section 12(5) Any determination that the requirement for Christian collective worship does not apply, shall be reviewed by

SACRE at any time on application by the head teacher and in any event after five years.

Section 13(1) Before appointing people to represent any denominations or associations as members of SACRE the LEA shall take all reasonable steps to assure themselves that they are representative of the denomination or associations in question.

Section 13(2) The LEA may remove a member 'if in the opinion of the authority he ceases to be representative of the denomination or associations which he was appointed to represent.'

Section 23 This section states the arrangements for LEAs to consider any complaint that the LEA or a school governing body has acted or is proposing to act unreasonably with regard, for example, to the curriculum or school worship.

Sections 84–88 These sections are about religious education and collective worship in grant-maintained schools.

Schedule 1 This schedule states the amendments to previous legislation relating to religious education which are made by the Education Reform Act 1988.

List of Recently Established Christian Schools

SUMMARY

Fifty-nine schools are listed below. Fifty-six of these were opened in the period 1978–1987. Of the other three, one was opened in 1969 and two in 1974. One of those opened in 1974 has now closed (East Sutherland School); the other two are still open.

Altogether, eleven of the fifty-nine schools listed have been closed.

The schools are listed in alphabetical order. Most of the information has been obtained from replies to the questionnaire which was first distributed in June 1987 with the help of Mr Stephen Dennett (then Headmaster, The King's School, Harpenden) and of Mr Arthur Roderick (Accelerated Christian Education, Hebron Hall, Dinas Powis, South Glamorgan CF6 4YB). In January 1988 a shorter questionnaire was sent direct to Christian schools which had not responded to the earlier one. The information was confirmed and updated where possible in summer 1989. All of the 48 schools listed and open supplied information.

Information about each school is in five sections, as follows:

1. Name of school.
2. Address.
3. Name of Head Teacher/Principal.
4. Date school opened (and closed where applicable).
5. Number of pupils on roll.

1. ABUNDANT LIFE SCHOOL
3. J Cairns
4. Opened 15 September 1986, now closed.
5. June 1987: 15

1. ACORN SCHOOL (Linked with Covenant School, Barking)
2. Hulse Avenue, Collier Row, Romford, Essex.
3. Miss Marion Rideout (Principal), Miss Susan Harvey (Head Teacher)
4. September 1980
5. June 1987: 35; June 1989: 51

1. BALLYMONEY INDEPENDENT CHRISTIAN SCHOOL
2. Market Street, Ballymoney, Co Antrim, Northern Ireland.
3. Miss M Keys
4. September 1983
5. June 1987: 25; February 1988: 31; June 1989: 47

1. BANGOR INDEPENDENT CHRISTIAN SCHOOL
2. 277 Clandeboye Road, Bangor, County Down, Northern Ireland, BT19 1AA
3. Mrs E P Rutherdale BA
4. September 1985
5. June 1987: 50; June 1989: 66

1. BARNSLEY CHRISTIAN SCHOOL
2. Fellowship House, Blucher Street, Barnsley, S70 1AP
3. Mr D Bavister
4. 22 September 1986
5. June 1987: 43; June 1989: 41

1. BEDFORD CHRISTIAN DAY SCHOOL
3. Susan Gerrard
4. Opened September 1979, closed 1983
5. September 1979: 3; February 1980: 6

1. BETHANY CHRISTIAN SCHOOL
4. Opened April 1983, Closed 1985
5. April 1983: 4

1. BETHANY SCHOOL
2. 215 Sharrowvale Road, Sheffield, S11 8ZB
3. Mr K Walze
4. September 1987
5. January 1988: 12; June 1989: 18

1. THE CEDARS
2. 219 Maidstone Road, Rochester, Kent
3. Mrs B Gross
4. 1969
5. June 1980: 40; June 1987: 81; June 1989: 80

1. THE CHRISTIAN FELLOWSHIP SCHOOL
2. 1 Princes Road. Liverpool L8 1TG
3. Mr Philip Williamson
4. January 1981
5. June 1987: 170; June 1989: 180

1. THE CHRISTIAN SCHOOL
2. South Lee Christian Centre, Baring Road, Lee, London SE12 0PW
3. Mr Peter Gregory
4. September 1986
5. June 1987: 94; January 1988: 126; June 1989: 140

1. CLOGHER VALLEY INDEPENDENT SCHOOL
2. c/o 13 Willend Crescent, Fivemiletown, Co Tyrone, Northern Ireland BT75 0QT
3. Miss Alison Pattison
4. September 1987
5. January 1988: 11; June 1989: 15

1. COLNE VALLEY CHRISTIAN SCHOOL
2. The Ramparts, Bakers Lane, Braiswick, Colchester CO4 5BB
3. Principal: Pastor F Wright, Head Teachers Mr C Vernon, Mrs L Eady
4. September 1985
5. June 1987: 30; January 1988: 46; June 1989: 48

1. COVENANT SCHOOL ·
2. Craigdale Hall, Craigdale Road, Romford, Essex
3. Miss M Rideout
4. September 1986
5. June 1987: 31; June 1989: 38

1. COVENANT CHRISTIAN SCHOOL, NORTHERN IRELAND
2. 17 Lisbane Gardens, Monkstown, Newtownabbey, Co Antrim BT37 0LD
3. Mrs Diane Whitla (Senior Teacher)
4. 1982
5. June 1987: 14

1. COVENANT CHRISTIAN SCHOOL, STOCKPORT
2. The Hawthorns, 48 Heaton Moor Road, Stockport, SK4 4NX
3. Dr R S Slack
4. September 1983
5. September 1983: 16; June 1987: 32; June 1989: 35

1. COVENTRY CHRISTIAN ACADEMY
3. Principal: The Rev John Pangle,
4. Opened September 1980, closed 1984
5. September 1980: 28; January 1983: 35

1. THE DOLPHIN SCHOOL
2. Church House. Holy Trinity Church, Brompton Road, London, SW7 1JA
3. Miss R Martin
4. January 1987
5. June 1987: 7; January 1988: 14; June 1989: 26

1. EAST SOLENT SCHOOL
3. Peter Phillips
4. Opened January 1985, now closed

1. EAST SUTHERLAND CHRISTIAN SCHOOL, SCOTLAND
4. Opened January 1974, closed 1981
5. 1977–8: 14; 1978–9: 20

1. EMMANUEL CHRISTIAN SCHOOL, FLEETWOOD
2. Elm Street, Fleetwood, Lancashire, FY7 6TJ
3. Rev Dr M B Smith
4. 1979
5. June 1987: 85; June 1989: 80

1. EMMAMUEL SCHOOL, NORWICH
3. E T Hopley Bsc CEng MIMechE
4. Opened 1984, closed 1987

1. FAITH CHRISTIAN ACADEMY
2. Hatchley Barn Road, Bromeswell, Suffolk, IP12 2PP
3. Pastor Greg Iehl
4. May 1979
5. June 1987: 10; June 1989: 23

1. FAITH CHRISTIAN SCHOOL
2. 3 Magpie Close, Thatcham, Berkshire RG13 4RZ
3. Mr T Dotson

4. September 1986
5. June 1987: 19; June 1989: 15

1. FAREHAM SCHOOL, SOUTHAMPTON (See East Solent School)

1. GRANGEWOOD INDEPENDENT SCHOOL
2. Chester Road, Forest Gate, London, E7 8QT
3. Mr S Sherwood
4. 1979
5. June 1987: 52; March 1988: 54; June 1989: 54

1. HALTON CHRISTIAN SCHOOL
3. Mr G T Hayden
4. Opened January 1986, closed July 1987

1. HANDSWORTH CHRISTIAN SCHOOL
2. 231 Handsworth Road, Sheffield, South Yorkshire S13
3. Mrs P E Arnott
4. September 1986
5. June 1987: 15; March 1988: 21

1. HIGHWAY CHRISTIAN SCHOOL (Formerly Shekinah Christian
   School)
2. Union Chapel, 255 Tooley Street, London, SE1
3. Mr K Dilliway
4. January 1982
5. June 1987: 65; March 1988: 72; September 1989: 60

1. HYFRYDLE CHRISTIAN SCHOOL
2. Hyfrydle Christian Centre, Hyfrydle Road, Talysarn,
   Gwynedd, North Wales
3. Mr D Rowlands
4. September 1985
5. June 1985: 5; June 1989: 8

1. KILSKERRY INDEPENDENT CHRISTIAN SCHOOL
2. 51 Old Junction Road, Kilskeery, County Tyrone, Northern
   Ireland BT78 3RN
3. Mrs Ann Foster
4. September 1979
5. January 1988: 48; June 1989: 48

1. THE KING OF KINGS SCHOOL
2. The King's House, 2 York Street, Manchester M1 7HL
3. Principal: Goos Vedder, Head: Mrs Brenda Lewis BEd

4. September 1986
5. June 1987: 13

1. THE KING'S SCHOOL, BASINGSTOKE
2. Sarum Hill, Basingstoke, Hampshire, RG21 1SR
3. Mr Richard Britton
4. September 1981
5. June 1987: 100; June 1989: 105

1. KING'S SCHOOL HARPENDEN
2. Elmfield, Ambrose Lane, Harpenden, Hertfordshire
   AL5 4DA
3. Principal: Mr David Barker. Head: Mr Keith Myners
4. September 1982
5. 1984–5: 200 in main school and 21 in nursery. June 1987: 156

1. THE KING'S SCHOOL, MILTON KEYNES
4. Opened 1983, closed 1987

1. THE KING'S SCHOOL, NOTTINGHAM
2. The Christian Centre, 104 Talbot Street, Nottingham, NG1
   5GL
3. Mr R Southey
4. September 1986
5. June 1987: 70; February 1988: 84; June 1989: 110

1. THE KING'S SCHOOL, SOUTHAMPTON (Senior School)
2. Fisher's Court, Main Road, Fisher's Pond, Eastleigh,
   Southampton SO5 7HG
3. Mr D G Trentham
4. 1985
5. 1986: 64; June 1987: 76; June 1989: 75

1. THE KING'S SCHOOL SOUTHAMPTON (Primary School)
2. 26 Quob Lane, West End, Southampton
3. Mr Douglas Williams
4. 1982
5. June 1987: c170; June 1989: 190

1. THE KING'S SCHOOL, WITNEY
2. New Yatt Road, Witney, Oxfordshire, OX8 6TA
3. Mr David W Freeman
4. September 1984
5. June 1987: 126; June 1989: 140

1. THE LANGLEY MANOR SCHOOL
2. St Mary's Road, Langley, Slough, Berkshire
3. Mrs S Eaton B Ed
4. September 1986
5. June 1987: 107 plus 26 under fives,June 1989: 220, plus 20 under fives

1. LIFE CHRISTIAN SCHOOL, BATTERSEA, LONDON
4. Opened September 1981, closed 1986
5. January 1985: 26

1. MOUNTAIN ASH SCHOOL
2. Oasis House, Essex Road, Chadwell Heath, Romford, Essex RM6 4JA
3. Mrs J Taylor
4. 1983
5. June 1987: 35; June 1989: 32

1. NEWCOURT CENTRE CHRISTIAN SCHOOL
2. 1–5 Regina Road, Finsbury Park, London N4 3PT
3. Mrs Susan Wisker
4. 1988

1. NEW LIFE SCHOOL
2. Maypole Road, East Grinstead, West Sussex
3. Mr K Jones
4. January 1986
5. June 1987: 16; June 1989: 36

1. NEW RIVER CHRISTIAN SCHOOL
2. Russell Road, London N 13
3. Mr Keith Lannon
4. 1985
5. June 1987: 43

1. NEW TESTAMENT BAPTIST SCHOOL
3. Pastor Jack Thrift
4. Opened September 1981, closed May 1982
5. 15

1. NEWTOWNABBEY INDEPENDENT CHRISTIAN SCHOOL
2. Ballyclare Road, Glengormley, Newtownabbey, County Antrim Northern Ireland
3. Mrs Joy Chambers

4. September 1983
5. June 1987: 31; February 1988: 35; June 1989: 45

1. OAK HILL SCHOOL
2. Okebourne Road, Brentry, Bristol
3. Mrs Ruth Deakin
4. September 1984
5. June 1987: 91; September 1989: 132

1. PENIEL ACADEMY
2. 49 Coxtie Green Road, Brentwood, Essex, CM14 5PS
3. The Rev M S B Reid
4. January 1982
5. June 1987: 69

1. PILGRIM CHRISTIAN SCHOOL
2. West Street Christian Centre, West Street, Dunstable, Bedfordshire LU6 1SX
3. Mr M C Skipper (Acting Head Teacher)
4. January 1981
5. June 1987: 51; June 1989: 57

1. REFORMED PRESBYTERIAN CHURCH SCHOOL
2. Archer Road, Ely, Cardiff, S Glamorgan
3. The Rev R Holst and The Rev David Lock
4. 1974
5. June 1987: 48; March 1988: 48; June 1989: 56

1. THE REGIUS SCHOOL
2. The King's Hall, 41a South Clerk Street, Edinburgh, EH8 9NZ
3. Mrs J Hutchinson
4. September 1986
5. June 1987: 5; March 1988: 12

1. THE RIVER SCHOOL
2. Oakfield House, Droitwich, Worcester, WR3 7ST
3. Mr T M D Crow MA
4. September 1985
5. June 1987: 108 plus 40 under fives; June 1989: 160 plus 50 under fives

1. SHEKINAH CHRISTIAN SCHOOL, TOWER HAMLETS
   (see Highway Christian School)

1. THE SHEPHERD'S SCHOOL
2. 71 Tressillian Road, Brockley, London SE4 1YA
3. Mr D Pott
4. March 1981
5. June 1987: 55; June 1989: 67

1. TREMORE CHRISTIAN SCHOOL
2. Tremore Manor, Bodmin, Cornwall, PL30 5JT
3. Miss Ann Whitaker
4. 1980
5. September 1983: 12; June 1987: 37; June 1989: 37

1. TRINITY SCHOOL, DUNDEE
2. 16 Bath Street, Broughty Ferry, Dundee, DD5 2PY
   (school meets on premises of St Peter's Free Church, Perth
   Road, Dundee.)
3. Mr S Will
4. August 1981
5. September 1984: 7; August 1985: 13; January 1988: 13;
   June 1989: 16

1. TRINITY SCHOOL,
2. Birkbeck Street, Stalybridge, Cheshire, SK15 1SH
3. Mrs S Baker
4. September 1978
5. June 1987: 85; September 1987: 95; January 1988: 100;
   June 1989: 100

1. VICTORY SCHOOL
2. Widcombe Hill, Bath, BA2 6AA
3. Pastor Allan Staggs
4. September 1987
5. September 1987: 9; June 1989: 14

1. THE VINE SCHOOL
2. Primrose Hill, Brentwood Essex
3. Mr R B Trace
4. September 1987
5. March 1988: 17; June 1989: 27

1. WYCLIF INDEPENDENT SCHOOL
2. c/o 8 Ffwrwm Road, Machen, Newport, Gwent, NP1 8NF
3. Mr A R Tamplin
4. September 1982
5. September 1982: 7; June 1987: 26; June 1989: 34

Further Extracts which Illustrate
some of the Thinking of those Involved
in recently established Christian Schools

'While this is contrary to the wishes of many parents, the assault on the Christian faith within the state system gathers momentum. In principle, parents have the right to withdraw their children from certain lessons on the ground of conscience, but these children are nevertheless indoctrinated day after day in a pattern of thinking which is humanistic in its presuppositions and approach.' (Davies, D.E. *Christian Schools* Evangelical Library of Wales and Association of Christian Teachers of Wales, 1978, p.42.)

'This radical divergence or cleavage in the human race results in two radically different, irreconcilable philosophies of life. These two philosophies of life may be broadly termed the secular and the Christian philosophies of life. The former is man—centred and holds that man as he exists today is normal; the latter is God—centred and holds that man as he exists today is abnormal (his life having been blighted by sin). . . . Education, then, must be either on a secular, non—Christian basis or on a Christian, God—centred basis. To obscure this distinction amounts virtually to abandoning the field to the non—Christian philosophy of life.' (Christian Parent—Teacher League Newsletter, March 1979, pp.7f.)

References

CHAPTER 1

1 *Education Act 1944 London*, HMSO, 1944, section 9(2).
2 *Social Trends 1987* p.56, Table 3.2.
3 Cruickshank, Marjorie. *Church and State in English Education 1870 to the present day* London, Macmillan, 1964, p.115.
4 *Ibid*. p.117.
5 *Ibid*. p.134.
6 Hilliard, F.H. *The Teacher and Religion* London, James Clarke, 1963, p.13.
7 *Ibid*. p.13.
8 Cruickshank *op.cit* p.143.
9 *Ibid*. p.141.
10 *Ibid*. p.141.
11 *Ibid*. p.138.
12 *Ibid*. p.138.
13 Jeffreys, M.V.C. *Education Christian or Pagan* London, University of London Press, 1946, p.17.
14 Clarke, F. *Education and Social Change* London, The Sheldon Press, 1940, p.v.
15 Livingstone, R. *The Future in Education* Cambridge, Cambridge University Press, 1941, p.110.
16 *Educational Reconstruction* London, HMSO, 1943, para. 36.
17 Ironmonger, F.A. *William Temple Archbishop of Canterbury his life and letters* London, Oxford University Press, 1948, p.571. Also quoted in Huxtable, John. *Church and State in Education* REP, 1963, p.8.
18 Ironmonger *op.cit* p.573.

19 Gower, Ralph 'Fight the good fight' in *RE News and Views* Spring 1987 p.6.
20 *Hansard* Fifth Series, House of Lords, Vol.132 (21 June 1944) Col.366. cf. pp.39f in the present book.
21 *Hansard* Fifth Series, House of Commons, Vol.424 (1 July 1946), Col.1803.
22 *Ibid.* Vol.424, Col.1810.
23 Cruickshank *op.cit* p.171.
24 *Hansard* Fifth Series, House of Commons, Vol.474 (4 May 1950), Col.1913.
25 *Social Trends* London, HMSO, 1987, p.56.
26 *Secondary Education For All: A New Drive* Government White paper, Cmnd. 604. London, HMSO, 1958, paras 2–5, p.3.
27 *Secondary Education For All: A New Drive* op. cit. pp.4f.
28 *Ibid.* pp.6f.
29 Taylor, G. & Saunders, J.B. *The Law of Education* 8th edition. Butterworth, 1976, p.46.
30 *Objective Fair and Balanced* London, British Humanist Association, 1975, pp.6f.
31 Counsel's opinion, as reported in the minutes of the Education Committee meeting on 11 June 1984.
32 *National Curriculum Consultative Document* London, DES, 1987. *Education Reform Bill* London, HMSO, 1987. cf. *Schools for the Future. The Government Proposals. Comments for Parents Staff Governors* London, National Association of Governors and Managers/London Diocesan Board for Schools, 1987. Lodge, B. 'Clergy fears opting out will close its schools' in *Times Educational Supplement* No.3725, 20 November 1987, p.3. Clare, John. 'Bishops say Bill threatens Catholic education' in *The Times* 17 February 1988, p.2.
33 *Education Reform Bill* London, HMSO, 1987.
34 Lodge, Bert. 'Churches find no solace' in *Times Educational Supplement* No.3726, 27 November 1987, p.5 and Hugill, Barry. 'Bishop's move — but which way?' in *Times Educational Supplement* No.3726, 27 November 1987, p.6.
35 Cruickshank *op. cit* p.172.
36 *Ibid.* p.174.
37 *Ibid.* Appendix C, p.192, Table V.
38 *Statistics of Education 1979* Schools Vol.1. London, HMSO, 1981, p.29. There were 39 pupils in this school in January 1983 — see O'Keeffe, Bernadette. *Faith, Culture and the Dual System A Comparative Study of Church and County Schools* London, The Falmer Press, 1986, p.11.
39 Rogers, Rick. 'Church schools — time to look again' in *Where* No.179, June 1982, p.7.
40 *Ibid.* p.6.
41 *Ibid.* p.7.
42 *Ibid.* p.7, Table 3.
43 *Ibid.* p.7, Table 2.
44 *Social Trends 1987* op. cit. pp.56f.

45 *The key to Christian Education. The Opportunity of the Church Training Colleges* London, The Press and Publications Board of the Church Assembly, n.d. p.4.

The Anglican colleges involved in teacher training and continuing in 1990 are:

   Canterbury, Christ Church College
   Carmarthen, Trinity College (Church in Wales)
   Cheltenham and Gloucester College of Higher Education (incorporating the College of St Paul and St Mary)
   Chester College (now affiliated to the University of Liverpool)
   Lancaster, St. Martin's
   Lincoln, Bishop Grosseteste
   Liverpool, St Katherine's College (now part of the Liverpool Institute of Higher Education)
   London, Whitelands College (now part of the Roehampton Institute)
   Plymouth, St. Mark and St. John
   Ripon and York St. John
   West Sussex Institute of Higher Education (maintained by a voluntary trust formed by Bishop Otter College, Chichester and West Sussex County Council)
   Winchester, King Alfred's College

The Roman Catholic colleges involved in teacher training and continuing in 1990 are:

   Birmingham, Newman College
   Leeds, Trinity and All Saints College
   Liverpool, Christ's and Notre Dame College (now part of Liverpool Institute of Higher Education)
   London, Digby Stuart College (now part of the Roehampton Institute)
   London (Twickenham), St. Mary's College
   Southampton, La Sainte Union College of Higher Education (cf *Catholic Directory 1987* Liverpool, Universe Publications Co Ltd, 1987, pp.490f.)

The Methodist Church founded two colleges: Westminster College, Oxford (formerly in London) is still a 'free standing' college, and Southlands College, Wimbledon is now part of the Roehampton Institute.

Congregationalists established Homerton College, Cambridge in 1852 and it still survives as a non-denominational voluntary college.

There is a substantial body of literature on Church Colleges. John Gay's *The Christian Campus? The Role of the English Churches in Higher Education* (Abingdon, Culham Educational Foundation, 1978) is an important contribution to the debate about their role and contains a useful bibliography.

46 O'Keeffe, B. *Faith, Culture and the Dual System* op. cit. pp.31f, 38f, & 59–66. cf Rogers, R. 'Denominational Schooling' in *NAME Journal* Vol.10, No.1, Autumn 1981, p.28.

47 Rogers, Rick. 'Separated brethren' in *The Guardian* 8 December
   1981, p.11; Rogers, R. 'Denominational Schooling' in *NAME Journal*
   Vol.10, No.1, Autumn 1981, pp.26–33; O'Keeffe, B. *Faith, Culture
   and the Dual System* op. cit.
48 Sherman, Jill. 'Shut down church schools says bishop' in *Times
   Educational Supplement* No.3656, 25 July 1986, p.1.
49 'Church schools offer power sacrifice' in *Times Educational Supplement* No.3407, 16 October 1981, p.3. 'The Allington Statement' (full
   text) in *ILEA Contact* Vol.10, Issue 18, 16 October 1981 p.6.
50 'Allington — one year on' in *Spectrum* Vol.15, No.3, Summer 1983,
   pp.27–29. There is a more detailed consideration of Christian
   Education in maintained church schools in chapter 3 of this present
   book.
51 *Times Educational Supplement* No. 3534, 23 March 1984, p.5.
52 *A Future in Partnership — a Green Paper for Discussion* London,
   National Society for Promoting Religious Education, 1984. Reported in *Church Times* No.6318, 16 March 1984, pp.1f, 20, and in
   Times Educational Supplement No.3533, 16 March 1984, p.1.
53 Gordon, P. and Lawton, D. *Curriculum Change in the Nineteenth and
   Twentieth Centuries* London, Hodder, 1978, p.1.
54 *Ibid.* p.47.
55 Department of Education and Science *Prospects and Problems for
   Religious Education* — the report of a seminar held at St. George's
   House Windsor in March 1969 London, HMSO, 1971, p.5.
56 MacIntyre, Alasdair. *Secularization and Moral Change* London,
   Oxford University Press, 1967, p.59.
57 Pointer, Roy. 'Church Growth in England?' in *Prospects for the
   Eighties* Vol.2. London, Marc Europe, 1983, p.7.
58 Martin, David. *The Religious and the Secular* London, Routledge &
   Kegan Paul, 1969, p.16 (This chapter previously published in *The
   Penguin Survey of Social Sciences* 1965).
59 Martin, David. *A General Theory of Secularization* Oxford, Basil
   Blackwell, 1978, p.3. cf. Hull, John M. *What Prevents Christian
   Adults from Learning?* London, SCM, 1985, ch.1 'Modernity and
   Christian education'. Hull accepts the importance and effect of
   secularization but takes care not to over state it, eg 'it is now
   increasingly recognized that secularization is but one aspect of
   the phenomenon (modernity), and although it is obvious that
   secularization has a direct bearing upon religion, other aspects
   of modernity may be just as important in influencing religious
   learning.' (p.3)
60 Wilson, Bryan. *Religion in Secular Society* London, Watts, 1966.
61 MacIntyre, Alasdair *op.cit.* pp.30f.
62 Lyon, David. *The Steeple's Shadow: on the Myths and Realities of
   Secularization* London, SPCK, 1985.
63 McIntyre, John. *Multiculture and Multi-faith Societies: Some Examinable
   Assumptions* The Farmington Institute for Christian Studies Occasional Paper No.3, n.d., p.3.
64 Martin, D. 1969 *op.cit* p.22.

65 Martin, D. 1978 *op.cit* p.viii.
66 Lyon, D. 1985 *op.cit* p.5.
67 Lyon, D. *ibid*. pp.10f.
68 Order of Christian Unity *Curriculum Christianity* London, Unity Press, 1977, p.23. cf. *The Fourth R* London, SPCK, 1970.
69 Lyon, D. 1985 *op.cit* p.22.
70 *Partnership in Christian Education* London, The Institute of Christian Education, 1962, p.43.
71 *Ibid*.
72 *Ibid*. pp.26f.
73 *Ibid*. p.26.
74 e.g. in date order: Hirst, P.H. 'Morals, religion and the maintained school' in *British Journal of Educational Studies* Vol.XIV, No.1, 1965.
   Wilson, J., Williams, N. and Sugarman, B. *Introduction to Moral Education* Harmondsworth, Penguin, 1967.
   'Religious Education and Moral Education' chapter 3 in *The Fourth R* (Durham Report). London, National Society and SPCK, 1970.
   Moral and Religious Education in County Schools Social Morality Council, 1970.
   Short, E. *Education in a Changing World* London, Pitman Publishing, 1971 esp. chapter 4 'Religion and Morality' pp.47–63.
   DES. *Prospects and Problems for Religious Education* London, HMSO, 1971, esp.p.8.
75 Short, E. *Education in a Changing World* op.cit. p.51.
76 *Ibid*. p.49.
77 Smith, J.W.D. 'How Christian can state schools be today?' in *Learning for Living* Vol.9, No.4, March 1970, p.8.
78 see pp.28–30. cf. p.50f. The major recent British sources on religious experience are: Robinson, E. *The Original Vision* Oxford, Religious Experience Research Unit, 1977.
   Robinson, E. *The Language of Mystery* London,SCM, 1987.
   Hardy, A. *The Spiritual Nature of Man* Clarendon Press, 1979.
   Hay, D. *Exploring Inner Space* Harmondsworth, Penguin, 1982; Oxford, Mowbray, 1987.
79 McPhail, P., Chapman, H. and Ungoed-Thomas, J.R. *Moral Education in the Secondary School* Longman, 1972 and associated pupil materials (cards, books and booklets) also published by Longman. Another example is 'Startline' (Schools Council Moral Education 8–13 Project).
80 Sankey, D. *Science, Religion and the School Curiculum a discussion paper* Oxford, The Farmington Institute for Christian Studies, 1983, p.2.
81 Short, E. 1971 op.cit. p.48.
82 Robinson, John A.T. *Honest to God* London, SCM, 1963.
   Robinson, John A.T. & Edwards, David L. *The Honest to God Debate* London, SCM, 1963.
   Packer, J.I. *Keep Yourselves From Idols. A Discussion of Honest to God* London, Church Book Room Press, 1963.
   Robinson, John A.T. But that I can't Believe! London, Collins, 1967.

83 Strawson, William. *Teachers and the New Theology* London, Epworth Press, 1969.
84 Goldman, Ronald. *Religious Thinking from Childhood to Adolescence* London, RKP, 1964 and *Readiness for Religion: a Basis for Developmental Religious Education* London, RKP, 1965.
85 Loukes, Harold. *Teenage Religion: An Enquiry Into Attitudes and Possibilities Among British Boys and Girls in Secondary Modern Schools* London, SCM, 1961 and *New Ground in Christian Education* London, SCM, 1965.
86 eg Howkins, K.G. *Religious Thinking and Religious Education: a critique of the research and conclusions of Dr. R. Goldman* London, Tyndale Press.
87 Schools Council Working Paper 36 *Religious Education in Secondary Schools* London, Evans/Methuen Educational, 1971, pp.30–34.
88 eg Newbiggin, L. 'Teaching religion in a secular, plural society' in *Learning for Living* Vol.17, No.2, Winter 1977, pp.82–88, reprinted in Hull, J.M. (ed) *New Directions in Religious Education* Basingstoke, Falmer Press, 1982. See also Sharpe, Eric J. 'Phenomenology and Commitment' in *Religious Studies Today* Volume 3, No.1, Autumn 1977, pp.2–5.
89 Mathews, H.F. *Revolution in Religious Education* Oxford, Religious Education Press, 1966.
90 Cox, E. *Problems and Possibilities for Religious Education* London, Hodder, 1983.
91 Gordon & Lawton 1978 *op.cit* p.73.
92 Department of Education and Science Circular 10/65 *Organisation of Secondary Education* 1965.
93 *Statistical Bulletin 6/84* DES, 1984.

Table 5 Pupils in maintained secondary schools
Percentage in each type of school January 1983

	%
Middle deemed secondary	7.0
Comprehensive	83.6
Modern	5.1
Grammar	3.1
Technical and other	1.1

cf. *Statistics of Education Schools 1982* DES, October 1983.

Table A1/82   Sheet 3   England   January 1982
Number of Secondary Schools

Comprehensive	3,358
Modern	357
Grammar	185
Technical and other	63

Number of Pupils in Secondary Schools

Comprehensive	3,150,313

Modern	211,367
Grammar	123,944
Technical and other	41,054

94 *Social Trends 1988* p.52, Table 3.4. This table gives the 1985 figure for pupils in comprehensive schools in Scotland as 96.4% and the 1986 figure for Wales as 98.5%.

95 Ree. H.A. *The Essential Grammar School* London, Geo. Harrap, 1956.

96 Cox, C.B. & Dyson, A.E. (eds.) *Fight for Education* (Black Paper One). London, The Critical Quarterly Society, 1969.
Cox, C.B. & Dyson, A.E. (eds.) *The Crisis in Education* (Black Paper Two). London, The Critical Quarterly Society, 1969.
Cox, C.B. & Dyson, A.E. (eds.) *Goodbye Mr. Short* (Black Paper Three). London, The Critical Quarterly Society, 1970.
Cox, C,B. & Boyson, Rhodes (eds.) *The Fight for Education — Black Paper 1975* London, J.M. Dent & Sons. Ltd., 1975.

97 Floud, J.E., Halsey, A.E. & Martin, F.M. *Social Class and Educational Opportunity* London, Heinemann, 1956.

98 O'Keeffe, Bernadette. *Faith, Culture and the Dual System* London, Falmer Press, 1986, p.33.

99 *Technical Education* Cmd. 9703. London, HMSO, 1956.

100 *Higher Technological Education* Report of a special committee appointed in April 1944. The chairman was The Right Hon. Lord Eustace Percy and the report is sometimes known as 'The Percy Report'.

101 Dutton, P. et al. *All Change* Microelectronics Education Programme/ National Extension College 1984.

102 Cox, E. 1983 *op.cit.* pp.23–25.

103 *Ibid.* p.23.

104 The *Education Reform Act* 1988 required the Secretary of State for Education and Science to appoint a National Curriculum Council to assume the responsibilities of the School Curriculum Development Committee and a Schools Examinations and Assessment Council to replace the Secondary Examinations Council.

CHAPTER 2

1 *Half our Future* London, HMSO, 1963, p.57. The statement quoted was made in the Newsom Report with reference to religious education in county schools, particularly the agreed syllabuses.

2 See Appendix 1 which sets out the provisions of these sections.

3 *Hansard* Fifth Series, House of Lords, Vol.132 (21 June 1944), col.366.

4 This point has been made in more detail in chapter 1, p.17.

5 *Northamptonshire Agreed Syllabus of Religious Education* (primary section). 1968, p.5.

6 Lord, E. & Bailey, Charles (eds.) *A Reader in Religious and Moral Education* London, SCM, 1973, p.3.

7 *Half our Future* op. cit. p.55. This tendency to regard Christianity as the main or exclusive content of religious education is also confirmed by an examination of the publications of the Institute of Christian Education and of the Student Christian Movement in Schools (which joined together in 1965 to form the Christian Education Movement).

8 Alves, Colin. *Religion and the Secondary School* London, SCM, 1968. One of the thirty members of the committee which produced this report was Dr. R.J. Goldman. His research had been into children's religious conceptual development: *Religious Thinking from Childhood to Adolescence* London, RKP, 1964 and *Readiness for Religion* London, RKP 1965. In this book there are further comments on Goldman's work in chapter 1, p.34.

9 *Ibid.* p.15. This taken for granted view of religious education is also clear in a 1967 National Society publication, which, for example, says: 'Religious education — teaching and learning about Christianity at school — is intended to help our children understand themselves and the world they live in.' *Education — Christian or Secular?* London, The National Society, p.2.

10 Alves *op.cit* p.158.

11 *Ibid.* p.158.

12 *Ibid.* p.14.

13 *Ibid.* p.148.

14 *Ibid.* pp.158f.

15 *Ibid.* pp.170–177.

16 Loukes, Harold. *Teenage Religion: An Enquiry Into Attitudes and Possibilities Among British Boys and Girls in Secondary Schools* London, SCM, pp.106–144.

17 *Ibid.* p.106.

18 Alves, Colin. *The Christian in Education London*, SCM, 1972.

19 *Newsom Report. Half our Future* London, HMSO, 1963.

20 Alves, C. 1972 *op.cit* p.43.

21 *Ibid.* p.44.

22 Schools Council Working Paper 36 *Religious Education in Secondary Schools* London, Evans/Methuen Educational, 1971. This Working Paper is considered in Alves, C. 1972 *op.cit* pp.53–59.

23 *Religious Education in Gloucestershire Schools* Agreed Syllabus of Religious Education. Gloucestershire Education Committee, 1981, p.2. This is an adoption of the Hampshire Agreed Syllabus 1978.

24 Scotland, Nigel. *The Changing Face of R.E* Leicester, UCCF, 1986, pp.44–48.

25 Tulloch, Frances (ed.). *Curriculum Christianity* London, Unity Press, 1977.

26 *Ibid.* p.63.

27 cf. chapter 1 of this book, p.15.

28 Daines, J.W. *An Enquiry Into the Methods and Effects of Religious Education in Sixth Forms* Nottingham, University of Nottingham Institute of Education, 1962.
Wright, D.S. *A Study of Religious Beliefs In Sixth Form Boys* Leeds, University of Leeds Institute of Education, 1962.

Gallup poll on television and religion (ABC Television) 1964.

Loukes, H. *New Ground In Christian Education* London, SCM, 1965.

Goldman, R.J. 'Do we want our children taught about God?' in *New Society* Vol.5, No.139, 27 May 1965, pp.8–10.

May, P.R. & Johnston, O.R. 'Parental attitudes to religious education in state schools' in *Durham Research Review* Vol.V, No.18, April 1967, pp.127–138.

Cox, E. *Sixth Form Religion* London, SCM, 1967.

Alves, C. *Religion and the Secondary School* London, SCM, 1968.

May, P.R. & Johnston, O.R. *Religion In Our Schools* London, Hodder & Stoughton, 1968.

Jones, C.M. *Worship In the Secondary School* Oxford, REP, 1969.

Religious Instruction and Education London, British Humanist Association, 1969.

Into the 70s A Discussion Document London, National Union of Teachers, 1969.

National Opinion Poll, March 1969. See Binyon, Michael 'More important than religion: sense of right and wrong' in *Times Educational Supplement* No.2814, 25 April 1969, p.1337.

29 Some relevant survey material from the 1970s and 1980s is found in the following:

McPhail, P. et al *Moral Education In the Secondary School* Longman, 1972.

May, P.R. 'Religious judgments in children and adolescents: a research report' in *Learning for Living* Vol.16, No.3, Spring 1977, pp.115–122.

Kay, W.K. *Religious Thinking, Attitudes and Personality Amongst Secondary Pupils in England and Ireland* Unpublished PhD thesis, University of Reading, 1981.

Souper, P. & Kay, W.K. *The School Assembly in Hampshire* University of Southampton, 1982.

'Whatever's Happened to God?' in *Womans Own* 26 September 1987, pp.20f.

This could be the subject of further research. Further investigation might confirm and perhaps account for the seemingly large number of such surveys in the 1960s and the apparent decline in the number of these surveys in the 1970s and 1980s.

30 Souper, P. & Kay W.K. *op.cit*

31 Swann Report. *Education For All* London, HMSO, 1985, chapter 8 'Religious education and the role of the school: religious education and the "separate" schools debate', pp.465–520.

32 Some inner city areas contain a number of people who are Hindus, Muslims or Sikhs. Whilst some of these people regard a Christian religious education as what they would expect in Britain, others feel that this kind of religious education might undermine their children's religious allegiance and hence they find difficulty in accepting it. In some parts of Britain, perhaps particularly the more rural areas, there are fewer people from the ethnic minorities and there may therefore be less hesitation about the continuance of a Christian religious education. In some cities, there are a number of West

Indians, many of whom come from Christian backgrounds, and they may well be happy with a Christian religious education.

33 Durham Report. *The Fourth R* London, National Society and SPCK, 1970.
34 *Ibid.* para. 214, cf. paras 114, 118 and 212.
35 Chapter 8 relates to this task.
36 It may be more justifiable because of consistency with foundation documents and because acceptable parental wishes should not be disregarded. It may be more advisable because in practice it can command the support of parents rather than their opposition.
37 Rossiter, Graham M. *An Interpretation of Normative Theory For Religious Education in Australian Schools* Unpublished PhD thesis, Macquarie University, 1983 (copy in Birmingham University Faculty of Education library), p.31.
38 *Ibid.* p.429.

CHAPTER 3

1 *The Fourth R* (Durham Report on Religious Education) London, SPCK, 1970, paras.439 & 440, p.206.
2 Dineen, Phil 'The shared school' in *The Tablet* 21 May 1983, pp.480–482.
3 Sallnow, Theresa 'Truly catholic schools' in *The Tablet* 8 October 1983, pp.977–979.
4 Currently stands at 85%.
5 cf. chapter 1, p.23.
6 cf. chapter 1, p.23.
7 cf. chapter 1, pp.22–24.
8 Lodge, Bert 'Questions of faith?' in *The Times Educational Supplement* No.3402, 11 September 1981. cf. O'Keeffe, B. *Faith, Culture and the Dual System* op. cit. pp.32f.
9 O'Keeffe, B. *Faith, Culture and the Dual System* op. cit. pp.20–23.
10 Rogers, Rick 'Separated brethren' in *The Guardian* 8 December 1981, p.11.
11 O'Keeffe, B. *Faith, Culture and the Dual System* op. cit. p.25.
12 *Ibid.* p.11 quoting publication of Christians Against Racism and Fascism.
13 Secondary Examinations Council, Working Paper 1 *Differentiated Assessment in GCSE* London, SEC, 1985, p.1.
14 *Universal Declaration of Human Rights* General Assembly of the United Nations, 1948, Article 26 (3).
15 Education Act 1980.
16 pp.73–91.
17 O'Keeffe, B. *Faith, Culture and the Dual System* op.cit. p.27. She also found one Anglican aided primary school which 'in theory gave priority to Christians' but 'there were no Christian children in the school — 98 per cent of the pupils were Muslims and 2 per cent

were Hindus and Sikhs.' (p.27) What Christian Education means in such a school could be the subject of further investigation.

18 pp.59–64.

19 O'Keeffe, B. *Faith, Culture and the Dual System* op.cit. p.29.

20 eg Durham Report *The Fourth R* op.cit. para 523, p.253.
Burgess, Henry. *The School in the Parish* London, Church Pastoral Aid Society, 1974, p.6.
Green, Ronald H. *Church of England Schools a Matter of Opinion* London, London & Southwark Diocesan Boards of education, 1983, p.4.
The Ethos of a Church School London, Southwark Diocesan Board of Education 1983.
Strudwick, C.V. et al *The Debate about Church Schools in the Oxford Diocese* n.d., p.22, para.75.
O'Keeffe, B. *Faith, Culture and the Dual System* op.cit. p.78.

21 Burgess, Henry. *ibid.* p.15.

22 Francis, Leslie J. *Assessing the Partnership* Abingdon, Culham Educational Foundation, 1984, Tables 5 and 7, pp.22f.

23 DES News Bulletin 196/87 *Kenneth Baker Consults on Collective Worship in Schools* London, Department of Education and Science, July 7 1987 and accompanying consultation letter. cf. House of Commons' Education, Science and Arts Committee Report *Achievement in Primary Schools* Session 1985–86, Third Report (Vol.1), 1986, paras. 6.42 — 6.44. The changes were included in the *Education Reform Bill 1987* London, HMSO, 1987 and in the *Education Reform Act 1988* (Section 6).

24 Hull, John M. *School Worship: An Obituary* London, SCM, 1975.

25 Keen, Geoffrey. 'The Allington statement' in *ILEA Contact* 16 October 1981, p.6, para 1(b).

26 *The Debate about Church Schools in the Oxford Diocese* op.cit. p.17, para. 57. cf. *Church Schools a Discussion Document* London, The Free Church Federal Council, 1984, p.5.

27 Todd, Noel. 'Church schools' in *Religious Studies Today* Vol.1, No.2, Spring 1976, p.2.

28 *Manual for Church Schools* London, The National Society, 1981, Notes for guidance, section 81/2 'School, church and community', para.7.

29 Chester. *A Guide to the Teaching of Religious Education for use in Church of England Aided Primary Schools* Chester, Diocese of Chester, 1987.

30 Todd, Noel. *op.cit* p.2.

31 Burgess, H. *op.cit* p.19. cf. O'Keeffe, B. *Faith, Culture and the Dual System* op.cit. pp.55–59, 67.

32 Alves, C. 'Religious education and the role of the church in society' in *Faith and Unity* January 1970, p.6.

33 *Worship in Church of England Primary Schools. A Guidelines Document* Diocese of Gloucester, n.d., p.8.

34 Burgess, H. *op.cit.* p.16.

35 *Ibid.* p.19.

36 *The Ethos of a Church School* op.cit. p.9.

37 Alves, C. 1970 *op.cit* p.7.

38 *Manual for Church Schools* op.cit. section 81/2, para 3.

39 Burgess, H. *op.cit* p.16.
40 Todd, N. *op.cit* p.2.
41 O'Keefe, Bernadette. 'Schools for all faiths' in *The Tablet* Vol.237, No.7454, 21 May 1983, Educational Supplement No.39, p.483. cf. O'Keeffe, B. *Faith, Culture and the Dual System* op. cit. p.37.
42 eg 'high academic achievement', mentioned by O'Keefe, B. in 'Schools for all faiths' *op.cit* p.483 and 'the concept of mission' mentioned by O'Keeffe, B. in *Faith, Culture and the Dual System* op. cit. pp.78f.
43 O'Keeffe, B. *Faith, Culture and the Dual System* op. cit. pp.22f, 26f & 39f.
44 *Ibid.* pp.23 & 27f.
45 Hirst, Paul H. 'Education, catechesis and the church school' in *British Journal of Religious Education* Vol.3, No.3, Spring 1981, pp.85–93.
46 *Ibid.* p.87.
47 *Ibid.* p.86.
48 *Ibid.* p.91.
49 *Ibid.* p.91.
50 eg Francis, Leslie J. *The Logic of Education, Theology, and the Church School* Abingdon, Culham Educational Foundation. 1983.

CHAPTER 4

1 *The Fourth R* London, National Society & SPCK, 1970, chapter 5, pp.153–168.
2 *Ibid.* p.153, para.341.
3 Rodgers, John. *The Old Public Schools of England* London, B.T. Batsford Ltd., 1938, p.8.
4 *Ibid.*
5 Edwards, D.L. *A History of King's School, Canterbury* London, Faber, 1957, pp.14f.
6 *The Fourth R* op. cit. pp.5, 154.
7 Carlisle Report *Partnership in Education. The Role of the Diocese* London, National Society & SPCK, 1971, p.46, para 79.
8 Dancy, J.C. *The Public Schools and the Future* London, Faber, 1963, p.68.
9 *The Fourth R* op. cit. p.156f, para 345, and p.161, para 351.
10 *Ibid.* p.156, para 343.
11 *The Fourth R* op. cit. p.166, para. 357.
12 *The Fourth R* op. cit. p.163, para. 354.
13 Souper, Patrick C. & Kay, William K. *Worship in the Independent Day School* University of Southampton, 1983, pp.29, 41–43.
14 *Ibid.* pp.28–32.

15 *The Fourth R* op. cit. p.161, para.351.
16 *Ibid.* p.163, para 355.
17 Carlisle Report *op.cit*
18 *Ibid.* p.46, para.81.
19 Dancy, J.C. *op.cit* p.69.
20 *Eastern Division:* Westwood House School, Peterborough; Cawston College, Norfolk; St. James' School, Grimsby.
   Midland Division: Denstone College; Ellesmere College; Worksop College; School of St Mary and St Anne, Abbots Bromley; St. Hilary's School, Alderley Edge, Cheshire; Smallwood Manor, Uttoxeter; Ranby House School, Retford; Prestfelde, Shrewsbury; Derby High School for Girls; St. Michael's College, Tenbury; The Bishop of Hereford's Bluecoat School.
   Northern Division: Queen Margaret's School, Escrick Park, York; Queen Ethelburga's School, Harrogate; Queen Mary's School, Hemsley, Nr. York; The King's School, Tynemouth; Waverley School, Huddersfield.
   Southern Division: Lancing College; Hurstpierpoint College; Ardingly College; Bloxham School; St. Michael's, Burton Park; Tudor Hall School, Banbury; The Archbishop Michael Ramsey School, Camberwell.
   Western Division: King's School, Taunton; Pyrland Hall, Taunton; School of St. Clare, Penzance; The Cathedral School, Llandaff; Grenville College, Bideford; St. Margaret's School, Exeter.
21 *The Woodard Corporation: Aims and Ideals* Ellesmere, The Woodard Corporation, 1985, p.1.
22 *Ibid.* pp.1f.
23 *Ibid.* p.3.
24 *Heirs and Rebels — Principles and Practicalities in Christian Education* Oxford, The Bloxham Project, 1982, p.11.
25 In date order:
   Hull, John M. *School Worship: An Obituary* London, SCM, 1975.
   The Child in the Church London, British Council of Churches, 1976.
   Hull, John M. 'From Christian nurture to religious education: the British experience' in *Religious Education* Vol.73, 1978, pp.124–143.
   Understanding Christian Nurture London, British Council of Churches, 1981.
   Hull, John M. 'Christian nurture and critical openness' in *Scottish Journal of Theology* Vol.34, 1981, pp.17–37.
   Hughes, Fred E. 'Religious Education and Christian Nurture' in *Religious Studies Today* Vol.11, No.3, Summer 1986, pp.2–4.
   Hughes, Fred. E. Editorial in *Religious Studies Today* Vol.12, No.2, Spring 1987, pp.2f.
   Freeman, Sid. 'Religious Education and Religious Nurture' in *Religious Studies Today* Vol.12, No.2, Spring 1987, pp.10–14.
26 Freeman, Sid. *Ibid.* p.10.
27 Chapter 3 Church Schools, p.65.
28 O'Keefe, Bernadette 'A balance for our schools' in *Journal of Beliefs and Values* Vol.7, No.2, 1986, p.5.

29 O'Keefe, Bernadette. Review of Francis, Leslie. *Partnership in Rural Education* London, Collins, 1986 in *Journal of Beliefs and Values* Vol.8, No.1, 1987, p.27: 'Unity of purpose among teachers can no longer be regarded as a distinguishing feature of church schools according to this particular study . . . just under half (48%) of teachers in voluntary aided schools said they had no real preference for teaching in a church school.'

30 *Op.cit* p.1.

31 Chapter 5 Christian Education in Recently Established Christian Schools, pp.73–91.

32 Goodliffe, J.B. *School Chaplain* London, Macmillan & Co. Ltd., 1961, pp.11–13.

33 *Ibid.* p.4.

34 *Ibid.* p.42, cf.p.72.

35 Dancy, J.C. *op. cit* p.67.

36 *Aspects of Worship in Boarding Schools* Oxford, Bloxham Project, 1970, p.15.

37 Richardson, Robin and Chapman, John. *Images of Life. Problems of Religious Belief and Human Relations in Schools* London, SCM, 1973, p.283.

38 Tonkin, Paul. 'Are we really a Christian nation?' in *Times Educational Supplement* No.3676, 12 December 1986, p.34.

CHAPTER 5

1 *Christian Parent–Teacher League Newsletter* March 1981, p.27.

2 *Christian Parent–Teacher League Newsletter* December 1980, pp.4f.

3 Some indication of these difficulties can be obtained from published HMI reports eg *DES Report by HMI on Coventry Christian Academy* Report No.229/83, p.16f. *DES Report by HMI on Acorn Independent School, Romford* Report No.110/84, p.5. *DES Report by HMI on Life Christian School, Battersea* Report No.162/85, pp.13,27.

4 Evans, Ross. 'Is it worth the effort?' in *Spectrum* Vol.16, No.1, Autumn 1983, pp.18–21.

5 Mohon, W.R. *Primary Curriculum* Publisher not stated, n.d., Introduction, p.1.

6 Davies, D.Eryl. *Christian Schools* Bridgend, Evangelical Library of Wales and Cardiff, Association of Christian Teachers of Wales, 1978, p.23.

7 Baker, Bruce. *Fathers and the Bringing up of Children* Mottram, Cheshire. Publisher not stated. n.d. p.7.

8 Harding, J.J. 'The "great debate" on education' in *Christian Parent–Teacher League Newsletter* January 1978, p.2.

9 Dale, Tony. *King's Educational Supplement* No.2, Spring 1985, p.3 in an article about Shekinah Christian School, Tower Hamlets. cf. Cook, Norman 'Christian education: a historical review' in *Spectrum* Vol.19, No.2, Summer 1987, p.113 eg: 'What is needed is a renewal

of the realisation that education is the proper concern of the church rather than that of the state.'

10 cf. Matthew 22.37, Luke 12.30.

11 cf. Psalm 78.1–8.

12 eg Proverbs 3.12, 22.15, 23.13, 29.15; Ephesians 6.4; Hebrews 12.5–11.

13 eg Deuteronomy 1.30f; Isaiah 49.5; Matthew 7.9–11.

14 eg Proverbs 13.22, 27.25–27, 31.27 and 2 Corinthians 12.14.

15 Ephesians 6.4; Colossians 3.21.

16 eg Proverbs 1.8, 6.20, 13.1; Ecclesiastes 12.1.

17 eg Deuteronomy 21.18–21; Ezekiel 18.10–13; Proverbs 20.20.

18 Hirst, Paul H. *Knowledge and the Curriculum* London, Routledge & Kegan Paul, 1974, p.26. Peters, R.S. *Ethics and Education* London, George Allen & Unwin, 1966, p.31 in 1970 edition. Schools Council Working Paper 53, *The Whole Curriculum 13–16* London, Evans/ Methuen Educational, 1975, p.44f.

19 eg Job.38–42, Psalm 8.3, 100.3, 139; John.1.1–3,9; Acts 17.24–28; Colossians 1.15–17; Hebrews 1.1–3.

20 See Holmes, Arthur. *Contours of a World View* Grand Rapids, Michigan, Wm. B. Eerdmans Publishing Co., 1983 and Peterson, Michael L. *Philosophy of Education: Issues and Options.* Leicester, Inter-Varsity Press, 1986, pp.20f.

21 Lyon, David. *The Steeple's Shadow* London, SPCK, 1985, p.132.

22 Romans 13.1–7; 1 Peter 2.13–17.

23 eg Isaiah 14.3–22; Daniel 3.1–23, 4.29, 6.16; Acts 4.1–22, 5.27–29, 16.35–39.

24 Colossians 4.16.

25 Ephesians 6.1–3; Colossians 3.20.

26 eg Matthew 19.13–15; Mark 10.13–16.

27 Nevertheless, teachers along with others can be held responsible under the Children and Young Persons Act, 1933 section 11, as amended by the Children and Young Persons (Amendment) Act 1952 section 8: 'If any person . . . having the custody, charge or care of any child under the age of twelve years, allows the child to be in any room containing an open fire grate or any heating appliance liable to cause injury to a person . . . not sufficiently protected . . . and by reason thereof the child is killed or suffers serious injury, he shall on summary conviction be liable to a fine not exceeding ten pounds.'

28 Barrell, G.R. & Partington, J.A. *Teachers and the Law* 6th edition, London, Methuen, 1985, p.371.

29 *Ibid. pp.371f.*

30 *Ibid.* p.372.

31 *King's Educational Supplement* Issue 4, Spring 1986, pp.10–12.

32 Pott, David. 'Teaching in three contexts' in *Spectrum* Vol.16, No.1, Autumn 1983, p.16. It should be noted that the use of corporal punishment in *maintained* schools has been prohibited since 1987 when section 47 of the Education (No.2) Act 1986 became effective. This to some extent reduces the degree to which the concept 'in loco

parentis' applies in maintained schools. The same Act increases the involvement of parents in maintained schools by its requirements regarding parent governors (section 3).

33 eg Isaiah 9:6, 63:16, 64:8; Matthew 5:45, 6:8,25–34, 7:9–11, 23:37.

34 eg Deuteronomy 32:4; Job 34.12; Isaiah 45:21; Zephaniah 3:5; 1 Peter 3:18; Revelation 15:3.

35 Barrell, G.R. *op.cit* p.28.

36 May, P. *Which Way to School?* Berkhamsted, Lion Publishing, 1972, pp.137–139.

37 Braithwaite, R.B. 'An empiricist's view of the nature of religious belief' in *Christian Ethics and Contemporary Philosophy* Ramsey, I.T. London, SCM, 1966.

38 *Is This For You?* London, British Humanist Association n.d., p.3.

39 Smoker, Barbara. *What's This Humanism?* London, BHA n.d., p.1.

40 *The World and you — A Humanist Perspective* London, BHA, n.d., p.1.

41 Bernstein, Basil. 'Open schools, open society?' in *New Society* 14 September 1967, pp.351–353, reprinted in Cosin, B.R. *School and Society* London, Routledge & Kegan Paul/Open University Press, 1971 and in Harris, A. et al (eds.). *Curriculum Innovation* London, Croom Helm/Open University Press, 1975. Blackham, H.J. *Humanism* Penguin 1968, second revised edition Hassocks, The Harvester Press/John Spiers, 1976, esp. Chapter 2 'The Open Mind' (pp.27–44) and Chapter 3 'The Open Society' (pp.45–64).

42 Stenhouse, L. 'The Humanities Curriculum Project' in *Journal of Curriculum Studies* Vol.1, No.1, November 1968, pp.26–33. Also Schools Council. *The Humanities Project: an Introduction* London, Heinemann Educational, 1970.

43 Peters, R.S. 'Reason and habit: the paradox of moral education' in Niblett, W.R. (ed.) *Moral Education in a Changing Society* London, Faber, 1963, p.51. Hirst, P.H. *Moral Education in a Secular Society* London, University of London Press, 1974, pp.44–52.

44 Hemming, James. *Individual Morality* London, Nelson, 1969, p.59, cf.p.51.

45 Lewis, C.S. 'The humanitarian theory of punishment' in Hooper, Walter (ed.) *First and Second Things. Essays on Theology and Ethics* London, Collins, 1985, pp.96–114.

46 Martin, Charles G. 'The case for state schools' in *Spectrum* Vol.16, No.1, Autumn 1983, p.23.

47 *Ibid.* p.24.

48 *King's Educational Supplement* Issue 1, Summer 1984, p.2.

49 Peter Davis was Head of The King's School, Basingstoke from its formation in 1981 until 1986 and when the *King's Educational Supplement* was launched in 1984 he was an Associate Editor. He was the first General Secretary of Christians in Education (until 31 December 1987). George Oliver was Inspector for RE in ILEA until 1986 and is now CIE Education Consultant. In *A Case for Christian Education* (1988 p.38) Dennett mentions *Partnership* which organization was intended to take over the function of the Christian Schools Advisory Service, the Association of Christian Schools

Heads and the Christian schools activities of CIE. Subsequently two
organisations were set up to help meet the needs of Christian
Schools: the Christian Schools' Trust and Christian Schools Cam-
paigns.
50 Storkey, Alan. 'The case for Christian schools' in *Spectrum* Vol.16,
No.1, Autumn 1983, p.10.

CHAPTER 6

1 Joslin, Roy. *Urban Harvest.* Welwyn, Evangelical Press, 1982, p.132.
cf. *Agreed Syllabus of Religious Instruction* City of Gloucester and
Gloucestershire Education Committees, 1962, p.182.
2 British Lessons Council. *Experience and Faith — A Christian Education
Syllabus with parallel themes for all age-groups in the Church.* London,
Methodist Youth Department/Nutfield, National Christian Education Council and Oxford, The Religious Education Press Ltd.,
1968, p.5.
3 *Ibid.* p.7. cf. *Partnership in Christian Education* (A Survey of the Day
school and Sunday school relationship) London, The Institute of
Christian Education, 1962 eg '. . . unless their pupils are brought
into the worshipping community of the church of their own choice
before they leave school, the bulk of the religious teaching and
inculcation of attitudes of worship as learnt at school will speedily
wither and die' (p.10) and '. . . men and women who see the
leading and building into the local worshipping community of the
instructed and challenged boy and girl as an essential priority in the
present field of Christian education'. (p.44)
4 Chapter 3, pp.60f.
5 Chapter 4, pp.67f.
6 British Lessons Council *op.cit* p.60.
7 pp.63–68, 74f, 85, 91–98.
8 eg Joslin *op.cit* pp.129–138.
9 Inglis, K.S. *Churches and the Working Classes in Victorian England*
London, Routledge & Kegan Paul, 1963, p.330.
10 Hull, John M. *What Prevents Christian Adults from Learning?* London,
SCM, 1985, p.8.
11 Joslin *op.cit* p.133.
12 *Ibid.* p.134.
13 *Ibid.* pp.135–137.
14 British Lessons Council *op.cit*
15 cf. p.116.
16 cf. p.116.
17 Joslin *op.cit* p.127.
18 *Ibid.* p.111.
19 Lush, Michael *All Age Activities for Learning and Worship* London,
Scripture Union, 1983, p.8.
20 Old, Margaret V. *Today's Children, Tomorrow's Church* London,
Scripture Union, 1974.

21 In Christian theology the value of human beings is indicated partly by their being created by God in his image. Further reference to the meaning of this is in chapter 8.
22 Hull, John M. *What Prevents Christian Adults from Learning?* London, SCM, 1985.
23 *Ibid.* pp.24–34.
24 *Ibid.* p.22.
25 pp.48–51.

CHAPTER 7 REFERENCES

1   Woodward, Peter. 'Bible Studies' in *Times Educational Supplement* No.3676, 12 December 1986, p.35.
2   *Ibid.* The book being reviewed when the comment in the text was written is: Gobbel, Roger and Gertrude. *The Bible: A Child's Playground* London, SCM Press, 1986.
3   *Ibid.*
4   *Partnership in Christian Education. A survey of the Day and Sunday School Relationship* London, The Institute of Christian Education, 1962.
5   See chapter 3 (pp.60f), chapter 4 (pp.67f), chapter 6 (p.93).
6   See chapter 3 (p.65), chapter 4 (p.70).
7   Hirst, P.H. 'Christian Education: A contradiction in terms?' in *Faith and Thought* Vol.99, No.1, October 1971, p.43.
8   *Ibid.* pp.43–54.
9   *Ibid.* p.46.
10 *Ibid.* p.48.
11 Hirst, P.H. 'Liberal Education and the nature of knowledge' in Archambault, R.D. (ed). *Philosophical Analysis and Education* London, Routledge and Kegan Paul, 1965, pp.113–138.
12 Hirst, P.H. *Knowledge and the Curriculum* London, Routledge and Kegan Paul, 1974, chapter 6, pp.84–100.
13 *Ibid* p.89.
14 Hirst, P.H. 'Christian Education : A contradiction in terms?' op.cit. p.44 and *Knowledge and the Curriculum* op.cit. p.84.
15 Hirst, P.H. 'Liberal Education and the nature of knowledge' op.cit. p.131.
16 Hirst, P.H. *Knowledge and the Curriculum* op.cit. p.48.
17 Hirst, P.H. 'Religion: A Form of Knowledge? A Reply.' in *Learning for Living* Vol.12, No.4, March 1973, pp.8–10.
18 Peters, R.S. *Ethics and Education* London, George Allen & Unwin, p.31 in 1970 edition. See also chapter 5 in this present book, p.79, ref.18.
19 Hirst, P.H. 'Christian Education: A contradiction in terms?' op.cit. p.44.
20 Their concern for education generally is an example, see for example this book pp.53, 90f, 109–117.
21 chapter 5, p.88f and chapter 8, p.112.

22 Acts 17.28.
23 Colossians 1.17.
24 Hirst, P.H. *Knowledge and the Curriculum* op.cit. p.25.
25 Hirst, P.H. 'Education, Catechesis and the Church School' in *British Journal of Religious Education* Vol.3, No.3, Spring 1981, pp.85–93 (which is an edited version of the author's Wiseman Lecture published in *The Oscotian*, 1978–9 issue).
26 Hirst, P.H. 'Christian Education: A contradiction in terms?' op.cit. p.43.
27 Hirst, P.H. 'Education, Catechesis and the Church School' op.cit pp.88ff.
28 *Ibid*. p.90.
29 *Ibid*. p.91.
30 *Ibid*. p.92.
31 *Ibid*. p.91.
32 *Ibid*. p.92.
33 *Ibid*. p.87.
34 *Ibid*. p.88.
35 *Ibid*. p.87.
36 *Ibid*. p.87.
37 Hirst, P.H. 'Liberal Education and the nature of knowledge' op.cit.
38 *Ibid*. in *Knowledge and the Curriculum* chapter 3, p.51.
39 *Ibid*. p.96.
40 Hirst, P.H. 'Education, Catechesis and the Church School' op.cit. p.90.
41 *Ibid*.
42 *Ibid*.
43 *Ibid*. p.93.
44 pp.100 and 104–107.
45 chapter 1, pp.27–31.
46 pp.113f.

CHAPTER 8 REFERENCES

1 Chapter 3, pp.62–64. cf O'Keeffe, B. *Faith, Culture and the Dual System* London, Falmer, 1986, pp.26–29.
2 Francis, Leslie J. *Religion in the Primary School. A Partnership Between Church and State?* London, Collins, 1987, p.52.
3 *Ibid*.
4 *Ibid*. p.58. The presence of denominational collective worship in county schools is illegal, according to the Education Act, 1944, section 26.
5 *Religious Education in Gloucestershire Schools*. Gloucester, Gloucestershire County Council, 1981, p.2. This is an adoption of the Hampshire Agreed Syllabus 1978.
6 *Op.cit* p.54.
7 *Ibid*. p.64.
8 *Ibid*. p.190.

9 *Ibid.* pp.43–45, 190.
10 eg Genesis 1.26f, 9.6; James 3.9.
11 eg Berkouwer, G. *Man: The Image of God* Michigan, Wm. B. Eerdmans, 1962.
    Cairns, D. *The Image of God in Man* London, SCM, 1953. Revised edition (with additional material by Jenkins, David) London, Collins, 1973.
    Clines, D.J.A. 'The image of God in man' in *Tyndale Bulletin* No.19, 1968, pp.53–103.
    Hoekema, Anthony A. *Created in God's Image* Michigan, Wm.B. Eerdmans/Exteter, The Paternoster Press, 1986.
    Rahner, Karl (ed.). 'Man (Anthropology)' in *Sacramentum Mundi: An Encyclopedia of Theology* London, Burns and Oates, Vol.3, 1969, pp.358–370.
    Robinson, Wheeler H. *The Christian Doctrine of Man* Edinburgh, T. & T. Clark, 1911.
12 cf. *Education Act 1944* London, HMSO, 1944, section 8(1)(b) and *Education Reform Act 1988* London, HMSO, 1988, section 1(2).
13 eg Genesis 3, Romans 5.12–14.
14 eg Genesis 9.6 and James 3.9 use the continuing image of God in man as a reason for the points they are making, thus implying that the image of God in man is not obliterated.
15 Chapter 5, p.87.
16 Ch.5 (p.89), ch.7 (p.103), ch.8 (pp.111f).
17 eg Matthew 18.11, 24.30, 26.64 cf. Psalm 8.4, Daniel 7.13.
18 Colossians 1.15.
19 1 Peter 2.22.
20 The Norwood Report *Curriculum and Examinations in Secondary Schools* London, HMSO, p.viii.
21 *Parental Influence at School London, HMSO, 1984, para 35, page 11.*
22 *Better Schools A Summary* London, DES, 1985, p.4.

Bibliography

Notes
1. Where a publication does not state an author it is listed under its title, discounting any definite or indefinite article.
2. Items published by a local education authority are listed under the name of the authority.
3. Items published by a particular diocese are listed under the name of the diocese (and also under the author on the few occasions where a separate author for a diocesan publication is also stated).

Adams, Jay E. *The Big Umbrella. The Christian School Teacher and His Disciples* Phillipsburg, Presbyterian and Reformed Publishing Co., 1977.

Adams, Jay E. *Back to the Blackboard. Design for a Biblical Christian School* Phillipsburg, Presbyterian and Reformed Publishing Co., 1982.

'Allington Statement' in *Contact* Vol.10, Issue 18, 16 October 1981, p.6.

'Allington Statement one year on' in *Spectrum* Vol.15, No.3, Summer 1983, pp.27–29.

Alves, Colin et al. *Religious and Moral Education. Some Proposals for County Schools by a Group of Christians and Humanists* Leicester, 1965.

Alves, Colin. *The Role of the Church Teacher Today* Westminster, Church Information Office, 1967.

Alves, Colin. *Religion and the Secondary School* London, Student Christian Movement, 1968.

Alves, Colin. 'Religious education and the role of the church in society' in *Faith and Unity* January 1970, pp.4–7.

Alves, Colin. *The Christian in Education* London, SCM, 1972.

Archambault, Reginald D. (ed.) *Philosophical Analysis and Education* London, Routledge and Kegan Paul, 1965.

Aspin, David. 'Church schools, RE and the multi-ethnic community' in *Journal of Philosophy of Education* Vol.17, No.2, 1983, pp.229–240.

Association of Christian Teachers. *Education with a Focus* Watford, ACT, 1983.

Astley, Jeff. *On Learning Religion: some Theological Issues in Christian Education* Durham, North of England Institute for Christian Education, 1984. Reprinted in *The Modern Churchman* Vol.XXIX, No.2, 1987, pp.26–34.

Astley, Jeff. Review of Peshkin, Alan. *God's Choice: The Total World of a Fundamentalist Christian School* (Chicago, University of Chicago Press), in *British Journal of Religious Education* Vol.10, No.2, Spring 1988, pp.111–113.

Aydon, Tanya and Endersbee, Mary. 'Another way to school' in *Today* September 1983, pp.54–57.

Baker, B. *Fathers and the Bringing up of Children* Mottram, Bruce Baker, 1978.

Baker, Glyn. 'Moral standards in education today as they affect parents, pupils and teachers' in *The Evangelical Magazine of Wales* Vol.18, No.4, August-September 1979, pp.11–14.

Baker, Kenneth. 'In the moral dimension' in *The Times* 1 February 1988, p.10.

Barrell, G.R. and Partintgton, J.A. *Teachers and the Law* sixth edition, London, Methuen, 1985.

Bates, Dennis. 'Ecumenism and religious education between the wars: the work of J.H. Oldham' in *British Journal of Religious Education* Vol.8, No.3, Summer 1986, pp.130–139.

Bath and Wells Diocese. *A Syllabus of Religious Education for use in Church of England Voluntary Aided Primary Schools in the Diocese of Bath and Wells* Bath and Wells Diocesan Education Committee, 1980.

Baumohl, Anton. *Ten Plus A Handbook for Teachers and Leaders Working With Tens to Thirteens in the Church* London, Scripture Union, 1981.

Beardmore, Len. 'A.C.E. schools "horrify" teacher' in *Elim Evangel* Vol.LXII, No.23, 13 June 1981, p.14.

Beardmore, Len. 'Christian schoools and their effect' in *Elim Evangel* Vol.LXII, No.32, 15 August 1981, p.7.

Berkouwer, G. *Man: The Image of God* Grand Rapids, Michigan, Wm. B. Eerdmans Publishing Company, 1962.

Bernstein, Basil. 'Open schools, open society?' in *New Society* 14 September 1967, pp.351–353.

Bingle, H.J.J. (ed.) *Christian Higher Education. The Contemporary Challenge* Potchefstroom, South Africa Institute for Reformational Studies, 1976.

Binyon, Michael.'More important than religion: sense of right and wrong' in *Times Educational Supplement* No.2814, 25 April 1969, p.1337.

Bishop of London. 'A Christian basis for English education' in *Theology* Vol.LXVIII, No.541, July 1965, pp. 327–332.

Blackham, H.J.(ed.) *Objections to Humanism* London, Constable, 1963.

Blackham. H.J. *Humanism* Penguin, 1968. Revised edition, Hassocks, The Harvester Press Ltd., 1976.

Blake, Nigel. 'Church schools, RE and the multi-ethnic community: a reply to David Aspin' in *Journal of Philosophy of Education* Vol.17, No.2, 1983, pp.241–250.

Blamires, Harry. *Repair the Ruins. Reflections on Education from the Christian Standpoint* London, Geoffrey Bles, 1950.

Bliss, Kathleen. *Christians and the Crowther report* (No.4 in 'Problems in Christian Education' series) London, The National Society, 1961.

Blomberg, D. 'If life is religion, can schools be neutral?' in *Journal of Christian Education* (Australia) Papers 67, July 1980, pp.5–20.

Bloxham Project Research Unit: *Some Approaches to Christian Education* Oxford, Bloxham Project, 1970.

——*Religious Education. Some Aspects of the Curriculum* Oxford, Bloxham Project, 1970.

——*Aspects of Worship in Boarding Schools* Oxford, Bloxham Project, 1970.

——*The School as Community* Oxford, Bloxham Project, 1970.

——*The Teacher and Christian Doctrine* Oxford, Bloxham Project, 1970.

Bloxham Project. *Heirs and Rebels – Principles and Practicalities in Christian Education* Oxford, Bloxham Project, 1982.

Boojarma, John. 'Needed: total parish education' in *Education Newsletter* (World Council of Churches) No.1, 1984, pp.7f.

Braithwaite, R.B. 'An empiricist's view of the nature of religious belief' in Ramsey, I.T.

Christian Ethics and Contemporary Philosophy London, SCM, 1966.

Breward, Ian. *Godless Schools? A Study of Protestant Reactions to Secular Education in New Zealand* Christchurch, Presbyterian Bookroom, 1967.

Bridger, F. *Children Finding Faith* London, Scripture Union, 1988.

Brighouse, Tim. 'Why Robin Hood needs to ride again' in *Times Educational Supplement* No.3678, 26 December 1986, p.4.

British Council of Churches. *The Child in the Church* London, BCC, 1976.

British Council of Churches. *Understanding Christian Nurture: A sequel to 'The Child in the Church'* London, BCC, 1981.

British Humanist Association. *Religious Instruction and Education* London, BHA, 1969.

British Humanist Association. *Objective Fair and Balanced* London, BHA, 1975.

British Humanist Association. *Is This For You?* London, BHA, n.d.

British Humanist Association. *The World and You – A Humanist Perspective* London, BHA, n.d.

British Lessons Council. *Experience and Faith – A Christian Education Syllabus With Parallel Themes For All Age-groups in the Church* London, Methodist Youth Department, Nutfield, National Christian Education Council and Oxford, The Religious Education Press Ltd., 1968.

Buren, Paul M. van 'Christian Education post morten Dei' in *Religious Education* (USA) Vol. LX, January 1965, pp.4–10.

Burgess, Henry James. *Enterprise in Education. The Story of the Work of the Established Church in the Education of the People Prior to 1870* London, National Society and SPCK, 1958.

Burgess, Henry. *The School in the Parish* London, Falcon/Church Pastoral Aid Society, 1974.

Burn, John and Hart, Colin. *The Crisis in Religious Education* London, The Educational Research Trust, 1988.

Cairns, D. *The Image of God in Man* London, SCM, 1953. Revised edition (with additional material by Jenkins, David) London, Collins, 1973.

Callan, Eamonn. 'McLaughlin on parental rights' in *Journal of Philosophy of Education* Vol.19, No.1, 1985, pp.111–118.

Caperon, John. 'Independent schools onward Christian scholars' in *Times Educational Supplement* No.3681, 16 January 1987, p.24.

Carroll, Eileen. 'Education and community' in *The Tablet* 19 February 1983, Educational Supplement No.38, pp.160f.

Carlisle Diocese. *Guidelines for Religious Education in Primary Schools* Carlisle Diocesan Education Committee, 1982.

Carlisle Report. *Partners in Education. The Role of the Diocese* London, National Society and SPCK, 1971.

Catherwood, Fred. *Education – a Better Way?* London, Association of Christian Teachers, 1977.

Catholic Education Council. *Evaluating the Distinctive Nature of a Catholic School* Bishops Conference of England and Wales, Department of Christian Doctrine and Formation, Co-ordinating Committee for In-Service, Evaluation and Appraisal in Catholic Schools, 1987.

Catholic Truth Society. *Declaration on Christian Education* Dublin, The Catholic Truth Society of Ireland Inc., n.d.

Chadwick, Priscilla and Gladwell, Maria. *Joint Schools A Discussion Document on Ecumenical Education* Norwich, Canterbury Press and Leominster, Fowler Wright Books, 1987.

Challinor, E.B. *The Story of St. Mary's College, Cheltenham* Cheltenham, Miss Challinor, n.d.

Chapman, Tom. *Christian Teachers in the New Era.* Report on conference at Preston on 27 September 1980.

Chelmsford Diocese. *Guidelines for Religious Education and Worship in Church Schools of the Diocese of Chelmsford* Chelmsford Diocesan Education Committee, 1977.

Chelmsford Diocese. *The School Curriculum – a Christian View.* Chelmsford, Chelmsford Diocesan Education Office, 1984.

Chester Diocese. *A Guide to the Teaching of Religious Education in Church of England Voluntary Aided Primary Schools* Chester Diocesan Education Association, 1987.

Cholmondeley, Essex. *The Story of Charlotte Mason* London, J. M. Dent & Sons Ltd., 1960.

'Christian Education and ecumenical faith' in *Education Newsletter* (World Council of Churches) No.2, 1983, pp. 1–3 and 11.

Christian Education Fellowship. *Secular and Christian Aims in Education* published by Christian Education Fellowship, n.d. This is a booklet reprint of 'Education secular and Christian' in *Christian Graduate* Vol.XVII, No. 1, March 1964, pp.1–9 and 'Christian aims in education' in *Christian Graduate* Vol.XVII, No. 2, June 1964, pp.15–24.

Christian Education Movement. *Christians Asking Questions About Education* London, CEM, 1977.

Christian Parent-Teacher League Newsletter 1978 to date.

Church Colleges Research Project, Interim Paper No.1, *The Future of the Anglican Colleges. A view from the Synod* The Board of Education and Diocesan Directors of Education. Abingdon, Culham Educational Foundation, 1984.

Church Colleges Research Project, Interim Paper No.2, *The Future of the Anglican Colleges. A View from Church Schools and Theological Colleges* Abingdon, Culham Educational Foundation, 1984.

Church Colleges Research Project, *Annexe to Interim Papers 1 & 2* Abingdon, Culham Educational Foundation, 1984.

Church Colleges Research Project, Interim Paper No.3, *The Future of the Anglican Colleges. A Preliminary Theological Critique* Abingdon, Culham Educational Foundation, 1985.

Church Colleges Research Project, Interim Paper No.4, *The Future of the Anglican Colleges. The First Year Students* Abingdon, Culham Educational Foundation, 1985.

Church Colleges Research Project, Interim Paper No.5, *The Future of the Anglican Colleges. The Third Year & PGCE Students* Abingdon, Culham Educational Foundation, 1985.

Church Colleges of Education. *Report of the Working Party on the Communication of the Christian Faith* London, Council of the Church Colleges of Education, 1966.

Church of England Board of Education. *The Church and the Newsom and Robbins Reports* London, Church of England Board of Education, 1964.

Church Statistics. Some Facts and Figures About the Church of England London, The Central Board of Finance of the Church of England, 1987.

Church Times articles: 'Priest's vision of ecumenical schools' in

Church Times No.6502, 25 September 1987, p.3 (review of Francis, Leslie *Religion in the Primary School: A Partnership Between Church and State?* London, Collins, 1987).

'Hope seen in new Church statistics' in *Church Times* No.6505, 16 October 1987, pp.1 & 20.

'Synod shares Board's concern over possible effects of the Education Bill' in *Church Times* No.6523, 19 February 1988, p.4.

Clare, John. 'Bishops say Bill threatens Catholic education' in *The Times* 17 February 1988, p.2.

Clarke, F. *Education and Social Change* London, The Sheldon Press, 1940.

Clines, D.J.A. 'The image of God in man' in *Tyndale Bulletin* No.19, 1968, pp.53–103.

Cockett, Michael (ed.) *RoSLA School and Christian Values* Southend-on-Sea, Mayhew-McCrimmon, 1972.

Conrad, R. 'A hermeneutic for Christian Education' in *Religious Education* Vol.81, No.3, Summer 1986, pp.392–400.

Coombs, Anthony. 'RE and sympathy' in *Times Educational Supplement* No.3737, 12 February 1988, p.4.

Cook, David. 'Educating Christians' in *Third Way* Vol.7, No.6, June 1984, p.8f.

Cook, Norman. 'Christian Education: a historical review' in *Spectrum* Vol. 19, No.2, summer 1987, pp.105–115.

Cook, Norman. 'A vision for Christian Education' in *Spectrum* Vol.21, No.1, Spring 1989, pp.45–55.

Copley, Terence. *Onward Christian Parents!* London, Church House Publishing, 1986.

Cosin, B.R. et al. *School and Society* London, Routledge & Kegan Paul/Open University Press, 1971.

Cousins, Peter. *Education and Christian Parents* London, Scripture Union, 1969.

Cousins, Peter. *Why we Should Keep Religion in our Schools* London, Falcon/Church Pastoral Aid Society, 1969.

Cox, C.B. & Dyson, A.E. (eds.) *Fight for Education* (Black Paper One). London, The Critical Quarterly Society, 1969.

Cox, C.B. & Dyson, A.E. (eds.) *The Crisis in Education* (Black Paper Two) London, The Critical Quarterly Society, 1969.

Cox, C.B. & Dyson, A.E. (eds.) *Goodbye Mr. Short* (Black Paper Three). London, The Critical Quarterly Society, 1970.

Cox, C.B. & Boyson, Rhodes (eds.) *The Fight for Education – Black Paper 1975* London, J.M. Dent & Sons Ltd., 1975.

Cox, E. *Sixth Form Religion* London, SCM, 1967.

Cox, E. *Problems and Possibilities for Religious Education* London, Hodder and Stoughton, 1983.

Cruickshank, Marjorie. *Church and State in English Education 1870 to the Present Day* London, Macmillan, 1964.

Cummings, David B. (ed.) *The Purpose of a Christ-Centred*

Education/The Purpose of a Christian School Phillipsburg, Presbyterian and Reformed, 1979.

Cunnington, Howard. 'Schools on the scales – church schools: outdated?' in *Christian Family* May 1987, pp.22f.

Daines, J.W. *An Enquiry into the Methods and Effects of Religious Education in Sixth Forms* University of Nottingham Institute of Education, 1962.

Dale, Tony. 'A brief history of Shekinah Christian School' in *The King's Educational Supplement* No.2, Spring 1985, p.3.

Dancy, J.C. *The Public Schools and the Future* London, Faber, 1963.

Davies, D. Eryl. *Christian Schools. Christianity and Education in Mid-nineteenth Century Wales and its Relevance for Today* Bridgend, Evangelical Library of Wales and Cardiff, Association of Christian Teachers of Wales, 1978.

Davies, Mervyn. 'The church's role in education' in *The Tablet Educational Supplement* No.40, 8 October 1983, pp.975–977.

Davies, Rupert E. (ed.) *An Approach to Christian Education* London, The Epworth Press, 1956.

Davies, Rupert E. *A Christian Theology of Education* Redhill, Denholm House Press, 1974.

De Graaff, Arnold H. & Olthuis, Jean (eds.) *Joy in Learning. An Integrated Curriculum for the Elementary School* Toronto, Ontario, Canada, Curriculum Development Centre, 1973, slightly expanded edition 1975.

De Jong, Norman. *Education in the Truth* Phillipsburg, Presbyterian and Reformed, 1974.

De Jong, Norman. *Philosophy of Education: A Christian Approach* Phillipsburg, Presbyterian and Reformed, 1977.

Deakin, Ruth. *Report on the New Independent Christian Schools* Bristol, Oak Hill School/Christians in Education, 1988.

Deakin, Ruth. *The New Christian Schools* Bristol, The Regius Press Ltd, 1989.

Deakin, Ruth. *New Christian Schools: the Case for Public Funding* Bristol, The Regius Press Ltd., 1989.

Dempster, L. 'Muslim parents back opting out' in *Times Educational Supplement* No.3725, 20 November 1987, p.12.

Dennett, Stephen. *A Case For Christian Education* Bradford, Harvestime Services Ltd., 1988.

Dent, H.C. *Century of Growth in English Education 1870–1970* London, Longman, 1970.

Department of Education and Science. Circular 10/65 *Organisation of Secondary Education* London, DES, 1965.

Department of Education and Science. *Prospects and Problems for Religious Education* (the report of a seminar held at St. George's House, Windsor in March 1969) London, HMSO, 1971.

Department of Education and Science. *Report by HM Inspectors* on *Coventry Christian Academy* Report No.229/83, London, DES, 1983.

Department of Education and Science. *Report by HM Inspectors on Acorn Independent School, Romford* Report No. 110/84, London, DES, 1984.

Department of Education and Science. *Statistical Bulletin 6/84* London, DES, 1984.

Department of Education and Science. *Report by HM Inspectors on Sir John Cass's Foundation and Red Coat Church of England Secondary School, City of London and Tower Hamlets* Report No.187/84, London, DES, 1984.

Department of Education and Science. *Report by HM Inspectors on Life Christian School, Battersea* Report No. 162/85, London, DES, 1985.

Department of Education and Science, *Better Schools A Summary* London, DES, 1985.

Department of Education and Science. *Kenneth Baker Consults on Collective Worship in Schools* DES News Bulletin 196/87, London, DES, 7 July 1987. Department of Education and Science. *The National Curriculum 5–16 A Consultation Document* London, DES, July 1987.

Dineen, Phil. 'The shared school' in *The Tablet* 21 May 1983, pp.480–482.

Douglas, Andrew M. *Church and School in Scotland* (The Chalmers Lectures 1982) Edinburgh, St. Andrew Press, 1985.

Dowman, Pamela. *Five Plus A Handbook for Teachers and Leaders Working With Fives to Sevens in the Church* London, Scripture Union, 1972.

Duke, Michael Hare and Whitton, Eric. *A Kind of Believing* London, Church Information Office, 1977.

Durham Report. *The Fourth R* London, SPCK, 1970.

Dutton, P., Nicholls, P. & Prestt, B. *All Change* Microelectronics Education Programme/National Extension College, 1984.

Editorial 'School – no place for God?' in *Polestar* No.44, February-March 1984, p.1.

Edmonds, Edward. 'Christian Education' in *School Chaplain's Encyclical* No.51, Autumn 1987, pp.13–18.

Education Act, 1944 London, HMSO, 1944.

Education Act 1980 London, HMSO, 1980.

Education (No.2) Act 1986 London, HMSO, 1986.

Education For All The Report of the Committee of Inquiry into the Education of Children from Ethnic Minority Groups (The Swann Report), Cmnd. 9453, London, HMSO, 1985.

Education For All A brief guide to the main issues of the Report. London, HMSO, 1985.

Education Reform Bill London, HMSO, 1987.

Education Statistics for the United Kingdom 1987 Edition London, HMSO, 1987.

Educational Reconstruction (Government White Paper) London, HMSO, 1943.

Edwards, D.L. *A history of King's School, Canterbury* London, Faber, 1957.

Eliot, T.S. *The Idea of a Christian Society* London, Faber, 1939.

Evans, Ross. 'Is it worth the effort?' in *Spectrum* Vol.16, No.1, Autumn 1983, pp.18–21.

Fair News October 1986 (p.7) and January 1987 (p.17). Each issue has a paragraph on Peniel Bible Assembly and its Christian school Peniel Academy.

Faith in the City. A Call for Action by Church and Nation (The Report of the Archbishop of Canterbury's Commission on Urban Priority Areas) London, Church House Publishing, 1985. Chapter 13 is entitled 'Education and Young People' (pp.293–324).

Farley, Edward. 'Does Christian Education need the Holy Spirit': Part 1 'The strange history of Christian paideia' *Religious Education* Vol.LX September 1965 pp.339–346. Part 2 'The work of the Spirit in Christian Education' *Religious Education* Vol.LX November 1965 pp.427–436,479.

Flannery, Austin (ed.) *Vatican Council II. The Conciliar and Post Conciliar Documents* USA, Costello Publishing Company Inc., 1975. ('Declaration on Christian Education', 28 October 1965, pp.725–737.)

Fleming Report. *The Public Schools and the General Educational System* London, HMSO, 1944.

Flood, Edmund. 'Getting adult formation started' in *The Tablet* 19 February 1983, Educational Supplement No.38, pp.159f.

Floud, J.E., Halsey, A.H. & Martin, F.M. *Social Class and Educational Opportunity* London, Heinemann, 1956.

Francis, Alan F. *The Place of Authority in Education* Cardiff, Association of Christian Teachers of Wales, 1976.

Francis, Leslie J. *The Logic of Education, Theology, and the Church School* Occasional Paper No.3 Abingdon, Culham Educational Foundation, 1983.

Francis, Leslie J. *Assessing the Partnership 1944–1984 An Interim Report on Religious Education, Assemblies and Church Primary Schools in Gloucestershire* Abingdon, Culham Educational Foundation, 1984.

Francis, Leslie, J. 'Denominational schools and pupil attitude towards Christianity' in *British Educational Research Journal* Vol.12, No.2, 1986, pp.145–151.

Francis Leslie, J. 'Roman Catholic secondary schools: falling rolls and pupil attitudes' in *Educational Studies* Vol.12, No.2, 1986, pp.119–127.

Francis, Leslie J. 'The influence of differing church aided school systems on pupil attitude towards religion' in *Research in Education* No.35, 1986, pp.7–12. Francis, Leslie J. *Making Contact. Christian Nurture, Family Worship and Church Growth* London, Collins, 1986.

Francis, Leslie J. *Partnership in Rural Education. Church Schools and Teacher Attitudes* London, Collins, 1986.

Francis, Leslie J. *Religion in the Primary School. A Partnership Between Church and State?* London, Collins, 1987.

Francis, Leslie J. and Rhymer, J. 'Roman Catholic secondary schools in Scotland and pupil attitude towards religion' in *Lumen Vitae* Vol.XL, 1985, No.1, pp.103–110.

Francis, Leslie J. and Egan, J. 'School ethos in Wales – the impact of non-practising Catholic and non-Catholic pupils on Catholic secondary schools' in *Lumen Vitae* Vol. XLI, 1986, No.2, pp.159–173.

Free Church Federal Council *Church schools: a Discussion Document Exploring Free Church Perspectives on Schools with a Religious Foundation within the Maintained Sector of Education* London, Free Church Federal Council, 1984.

Freeman, Sid. 'Religious Education and religious nurture' in *Religious Studies Today* Vol.12, No.2, Spring 1987, pp.10–14.

Freer, Brian. *Teaching Sunday School* Welwyn, Evangelical Press, 1984.

Fuller, Edmund (ed.) *The Christian Idea of Education* New Haven, Yale Unmiversity Press, 1957.

A Future in Partnership – a Green Paper for Discussion London, National Society for Promoting Religious Education, 1984.

Gathorne-Hardy, Jonathan *The Public School Phenomenon 597–1977* London, Hodder & Stoughton, 1977.

Gay, Brenda M. *The Church of England and the Independent Schools* Abingdon, Culham Educational Foundation, 1985.

Gay, John D. *Between Church and Chalkface* Occasional Paper No.6. Abingdon, Culham Educational Foundation, 1985.

Gay, John D. *The Size of Anglican Primary Schools* Culham College Institute Occasional Paper No.7 Abingdon, Culham Educational Foundation, 1985.

Gay, John D. et al *The Future of the Anglican Colleges of Higher Education* (Final report of the Church Colleges Research Project) Abingdon, Culham College Institute, 1986.

General Synod Board of Education *Children in The Way New Directions for the Church's Children* London, The National Society and Church House Publishing, 1988.

Gloucester Diocese *Worship in Church of England Primary Schools. A Guidelines Document* Gloucester Diocesan Education Committee, 1987.

Gloucester *Agreed Syllabus of Religious Instruction* Gloucester, City of Gloucester and Gloucestershire Education Committees, 1962.

Gloucestershire Agreed Syllabus of Religious Education *Religious Education in Gloucestershire Schools* Gloucestershire Education Committee, 1981.

Goldman, Ronald J *Religious Thinking from Childhood to Adolescence* London, RKP, 1964.

Goldman, Ronald J *Readiness for Religion: A Basis for Developmental Religious Education* London, RKP, 1965.

Goldman, Ronald J. 'Do we want our children taught about God?' in *New Society* Vol.5, No.139, 27 May 1965, pp.8–10.

Goodliffe, J.B *School Chaplain* London, Macmillan & Co. Ltd., 1961.

Gordon, Peter & Lawton, Denis *Curriculum Change in the Nineteenth and Twentieth Centuries* Hodder, 1978.

Gower, Ralph *Religious Education in the Infant Years* Tring, Lion Publishing, 1982.

Gower, Ralph *Religious Education in the Junior Years* Tring, Lion Publishing, 1984.

Gower, Ralph. 'Fight the good fight' in *RE News and Views* Vol.4, No.2, Spring 1987, pp.6f.

Graham, Andy. 'The scope of Christian Education' in *Elim Evangel* Vol.LXVII, No.36, 6 September 1986, pp.6f.

Green, Ronald H *Church of England Church Schools — a Matter of Opinion* London, Schools Division of the London & Southwark Diocesan Boards of Education, 1983.

Gresham Machen, J *Education, Christianity and the State* Maryland, USA, The Trinity Foundation, 1987.

Grimmitt, M. 'When is commitment a problem in religious education?' *British Journal of Educational Studies* Vol.29, No.1, February 1981, pp.42–53.

Groome, Thomas H *Christian Religious Education* San Francisco, Harper & Row, 1980.

Guildford Diocese *Diocesan Syllabus Guidelines for Religious Education* Diocese of Guildford Education Department, n.d.

Hadley, G.V.S. 'The Christian independent school: a response' in *Journal of Christian Education* Papers 75, November 1982, pp.18–23.

Half Our Future A Report of the Central Advisory Council for Education (England). London, HMSO, 1963.

Hansard House of Commons, Fifth Series, Vol.424, 1 July 1946, cols.1802–1859 and Vol.474, 4 May 1950, cols.1908–1975.

Hansard House of Commons, Sixth Series, Vol. 121, No.30, 26 October 1987, cols.81–118; Vol.123, No.55, 1 December 1987, cols.769–868; Vol. 123, No.58, 4 December 1987, cols.1278–1282; Vol. 128, No.105, 29 February 1988, cols.791–798.

Hansard House of Lords, Fifth Series, Vol.132, col. 306 (21 June 1944) — col.607 (29 June 1944); Vol.379, Nos.29 and 30, 16 February 1977, cols.1653–1735; Vol.383, Nos. 68 and 69, 18 May 1977, cols. 702–721 & 727–874; Vol. 492, No. 71, 4 February 1988, cols.1187–1190; Vol.493, No.85, 26 February 1988, cols.1453–1486.

Harding, J.J. 'Why we need Christian day-schools' in *Spectrum* Vol.2, No.3, May 1970, pp.100f.

Harding, J.J. 'The "great debate" on education' in *Christian Parent–Teacher League Newsletter* January 1978, p.2.

Hardy, A *The Spiritual Nature of Man* Oxford, Clarendon Press, 1979.

Hardy, Daniel W. 'The implications of pluralism for religious education' in *Learning for Living* Vol.16, No.2, Winter, 1976.

Hardy, Daniel W. 'Truth in religious education: further reflections on the implications of pluralism' in *British Journal of Religious education* Vol.1, No.3, Spring 1979, pp.102–107, 119.

Harris, A. et al (eds.) *Curriculum Innovation* London, Croom Helm/Open University Press, 1975.

Harte, David. 'Education and the Law' chapter 3 (pp.64–93) in Kaye, Bruce *Obeying Christ in a Changing World* Vol.3 of *The Changing World* London, Collins, 1977.

Hawkes, Adrian. 'Good response to New Court's Christian day school plan' in *Elim Evangel* Vol.LXII, No.19, 9 May 1981, p.3.

Hay, D *Exploring Inner Space* Harmondsworth, Penguin, 1982 and Oxford, Mowbray 1987.

Haynes, David *Models in Physics* (No.4 in The Bloxham Project 'Models in science and religion' series). Bloxham Project, 1984.

Hearn, B.W *Religious Education and the Primary Teacher* London, Pitman, 1974.

Heeney, Brian *Mission to the Middle Classes The Woodard Schools 1848–1891* London, SPCK, 1969.

Hellier, Graham *Models of God* (No.5 in The Bloxham Project 'Models in science and religion' series). Bloxham Project, 1984.

Hemming, James *Individual Morality* London, Thomas Nelson & Sons Ltd., 1969.

Hereford Diocese. See Hunt, M. & Colquhoun, H.

Heywood, David *Theology or Social Science? The Theoretical Basis for Christian Education* Durham, North of England Institute for Christian Education, 1986.

Heywood, David. 'Christian Education as enculturation' in *British Journal of Religious Education* Vol.10, No.2, Spring 1988, pp.65–71.

Higher Technological Education London, HMSO, 1945 (sometimes known as 'The Percy Report' after the Chairman of the Committee, The Right Hon. Lord Eustace Percy).

Hill, Brian V *Called to Teach — the Christian Presence in Australian Education* Sydney and London, Angus and Robertson, 1971.

Hill, B. V. 'Is it time we deschooled Christianity?' in *Journal of Christian Education* Papers 63, November 1978, pp.5–21.

Hill, Brian V. 'Teacher commitment and the ethics of teaching for commitment' in *Religious Education* Vol.76, No.3, May-June 1981, pp.322–336.

Hill, Brian V *Faith at the Blackboard. Issues Facing the Christian teacher* Michigan, William B. Eerdmans, 1982.

Hill, Brian V. 'Christian schools: issues to be resolved' in *Journal of Christian Education* Papers 75, November 1982, pp.5–17.

Hill, Brian V *The Greening of Christian Education* Homebush West, NSW, Australia, Lancer Books, 1985.

Hilliard, F.H *The Teacher and Religion* London, James Clarke, 1963.

Hilliard, F.H. et al *Christianity in Education* (The Hibbert lectures 1965) London, George Allen & Unwin Ltd, 1966.

Hirst, Paul H. 'Liberal Education and the nature of knowledge' in Archambault, R. D *Philosophical Analysis and Education* London, RKP, 1965, pp.113–138.

Hirst, Paul H. 'Morals, religion and the maintained school' in *British Journal of Educational Studies* Vol.XIV, No.1, November 1965, pp.5–18.

Hirst, Paul H. 'Christian Education: a contradiction in terms?' *Faith and Thought* Vol.99, No.1, October 1971, pp.43–54 and *Learning for Living* Vol.11, No.4, March 1972, pp.6–10.

Hirst, Paul H. 'Religion: a form of knowledge? A reply' in *Learning for Living* Vol.12, No.4. March 1973, pp.8–10.

Hirst, Paul H *Knowledge and the Curriculum* London, Routledge & Kegan Paul, 1974.

Hirst, Paul H *Moral Education in a Secular Society* London, University of London Press, 1974.

Hirst, Paul H. 'Religious beliefs and educational principles' *Learning for Living* Vol.15, No.4, Summer 1976, pp.155–157.

Hirst, Paul H. 'Education, catechesis and the church school' in *British Journal of Religious Education* Vol.3, No.3, Spring 1981, pp.85–93.

Hodgson, Peter *Models in Science and Theology* (No.2 in The Bloxham Project 'Models in science and religion'series). Bloxham Project, 1984.

Hodgson, Peter *Models in Physics* (No.7 in The Bloxham Project 'Models in science and religion' series). Bloxham Project, 1984.

Hoekema, Anthony *Created in God's Image* Michigan, Wm. B. Eerdmans and Exeter, The Paternoster Press, 1986.

Hogg, Anna C. 'Christians and schools' *Journal of Christian Education* Papers 67, July 1980, pp.45–56.

Holm, Jean L *Teaching Religion in School: A Practical Approach* London, Oxford University Press, 1975.

Holmes, Arthur F *Contours of a World View* Michigan, Wm. B. Eerdmans, 1983.

Holmes, Arthur F *The Idea of a Christian College* Michigan, Wm. B. Eerdmans, Second edition, 1987.

Hooper, Walter (ed.) *First and Second Things. Essays on Theology and Ethics* London, Collins, 1985.

House of Commons' Education, Science and Arts Committee Report *Achievement in Primary Schools* Session 1985–86. Third Report (Vol.1), 1986.

Howard, Donald R *Rebirth of our Nation* Lewisville, Texas, Accelerated Christian Education, 1979.

Howard, Donald R *American Educational Reform of the 80s* Lewisville, Texas, Accelerated Christian Education, 1982.

Howard, Donald R *The Great Commandment* Texas, Accelerated Christian Education, 1983.

Howard, Donald R *The Strengths and Weaknesses of the A.C.E. Program* Texas, Accelerated Christian Education, 1985.

Howkins, Kenneth C *Religious Thinking and Religious Education: A Critique of the Research and Conclusions of Dr. R. Goldman* London, Tyndale Press, 1966 and Third edition, Leicester, Theological Students Fellowship, 1977.

Hubery, Douglas S *The Experiential Approach to Christian Education* London, Chester House Publications and Redhill, Denholm House Press, 1960.

Hubery, Douglas S *Teaching the Christian Faith Today* Redhill, National Sunday School Union, 1965.

Hubery, Douglas S *Christian Education and the Bible* Redhill, National Christian Education Council, 1967.

Hubery, Douglas S *Christian Education in State and Church* Redhill, Denholm House Press, 1972.

Hudspeth, Sally *What About the Children?* Eastbourne, Kingsway Publications, 1987.

Hughes, Fred *Whose Child?* Cardiff, Association of Christian Teachers of Wales, 1982.

Hughes, Fred. 'The Aims of Education' in *Spectrum* Vol.15, No.3, Summer 1983, pp.7–11.

Hughes, Fred. and Kay, William K. 'Christian light on education' in *Religious Education* Vol.80, No.1, Winter 1985, pp.51–63.

Hughes, Fred. 'Religious Education and Christian nurture' in *Religious Studies Today* Vol.11, No.3, Summer 1986, pp.2–4.

Hughes, Fred. 'Whatever is happening to RE?' in *21st Century Christian* February 1988, pp.36–39.

Hughes, Fred. 'Christian Concern for Education' in Shaw, Ian. (ed) *Social Issues and the Local Church* Bridgend, Evangelical Press of Wales, 1988, pp.105–118.

Hughes, Fred. 'Talking About Christian Education' in *The Chaplain's Encyclical* No.54, Winter 1989, pp.2–5.

Hughes, Fred. 'Christian Education Under Review' in *Spectrum* Vol.21, No.2, Summer 1989, pp.121–129.

Hugill, Barry. 'Bishop's move — but which way?' in *Times Educational Supplement* No.3726, 27 November 1987, p.6.

Hugill, Barry. 'Cross purpose. Will Mr Baker answer the Christian schools' prayers?' in *Times Educational Supplement* No.3795, 24 March 1989, p.18.

Hull, John M *School Worship: An Obituary* London, SCM, 1975.

Hull, John M. 'Christian theology and educational theory: can there be connections?' *British Journal of Educational Studies* Vol.24, No.2, June 1976, pp.127–143.

Hull, John M. 'What is theology of education?' in *Scottish Journal of Theology* Vol.30, 1977, pp.3–29.

Hull, John M. 'From Christian nurture to religious education;

the British experience' in *Religious Education* Vol.73, 1978, pp.124–143.

Hull, John M. 'Christian nurture and critical openness' in *Scottish Journal of Theology* Vol.34, 1981, pp.17–37.

Hull, John M *What Prevents Christian adults from learning?* London, SCM, 1985.

Hunt, Margaret and Colquhoun, Helen *Signposts for a Journey. Religious Education Themes for Young Children* Hereford Diocesan Council for Education, 1980.

Hutchinson, James. 'Education that is Christian' in *Elim Evangel* Vol.LXVII, No.36, 6 September 1986, p.3.

Huxtable, John *Church and State in Education* Religious Education Press, 1963.

Inglis, K.S *Churches and the Working Classes in Victorian England* London, Routledge and Kegan Paul, 1963.

Institute of Christian Education *Religious Education in Schools* The Report of an Inquiry made by the Research Committee of the Institute of Christian Education into the working of the 1944 Education Act. Revised edition, London, National Society and SPCK, 1957. First published 1954.

Institute of Christian Education *Partnership in Christian Education. A Survey of the Day School and Sunday School Relationship* London, The Institute of Christian Education, 1962.

Ironmonger, F.A *William Temple Archbishop of Canterbury his Life and Letters* London, Oxford University Press, 1948.

Jeffreys, M.V.C *Education Christian or Pagan* London, University of London Press, 1946.

Jeffreys, M.V.C *Glaucon an Inquiry Into the Aims of Education* London, Sir Isaac Pitman & Sons Ltd., 1950, revised edition, 1955.

Jeffreys, M.V.C *Personal Values in the Modern World* Harmondsworth, Penguin, 1962.

Jeffreys, M.V.C *The Unity of Education* Wallington, The Religious Education Press Ltd., 1966.

Jeffreys, M.V.C *The Ministry of Teaching* London, Sir Isaac Pitman & Sons Ltd., 1967.

Jeffreys, M.V.C *Truth is not Neutral. A study of Freedom and Authority in Religious Education* Oxford, The Religious Education Press Ltd., 1969.

Johnson, Daphne *Private Schools and State Schools: Two Systems or One?* Milton Keynes, Oxford University Press, 1987.

Johnson, O.R *Christianity in a Collapsing Culture* Exeter, The Paternoster Press, 1976.

Jones, Clifford M *The Methods of Christian Education* London, SCM, 1949.

Jones, Clifford M *Pioneering in Christian Education. The British Lessons Council 1916–1966* Wallington, The Religious Education Press Ltd., 1966.

Jones, Clifford M *Worship in the Secondary School* REP, 1969.

Jones, Deborah M *Focus on Faith. A Guide on the Path to Catholic Christianity* Bury St Edmunds, Kevin Mayhew Ltd., 1987.

Jones, Denis. 'The Allington Statement' in *Spectrum* Vol.15, No.33, Summer 1983, pp.27–29.

Jones, R.M. and Davies, Gwyn *The Christian Heritage of Welsh Education* Bridgend, Evangelical Press of Wales, 1986.

Joslin, Roy *Urban Harvest* Welwyn, Evangelical Press, 1982.

Kay, William K *Religious Thinking, Attitudes and Personality Amongst Secondary Pupils in England and Ireland* Unpublished PhD thesis, University of Reading 1981.

Kay, William K. 'Philosophical and cultural bearings on the curriculum and religious studies' in *Educational Studies* (Abingdon) Vol.8, No.2, 1982, pp.123–129.

Kay, William K. 'The Church and Education' in *Spectrum* Vol.21, No.1, Spring 1989, pp.39–43.

Kaye, Bruce *Obeying Christ in a Changing World* Vol.3: *The Changing World* London, Collins, 1977. Prepared for the second National Evangelical Anglican Congress 1977.

The Key to Christian Education. The Opportunity of the Church Training Colleges London, The Press and Publications Board of the Church Assembly, n.d.

Kibble, David G. 'Religious Studies and the quest for truth' in *British Journal of Educational Studies* Vol.24, No.2, June 1976, pp.144–154.

Kibble, David G. 'From theology to School Council' in *Learning for Living* Vol.17, No.4, Summer 1978, pp.163–166.

King's Educational Supplement 1984 to date.

Kirk, K.E *The Story of the Woodard schols* London, Hodder & Stoughton, 1937.

Krannendonk, D.L *Christian Day Schools: Why and How* Ontario, Canada, Paideia Press, 1978.

Langley, Bob. 'Church, home and school: a partnership?' in *Review*, March 1980, pp.11–14.

Lawlor, Sheila. 'An answer to the bishops' in *The Tablet* Vol.242, No.7701, 20 February 1988, Educational Supplement No.53, pp.204–206.

Lawson, John & Silver, Harold *A Social History of Education in England* London, Methuen, 1973.

Leavey, Carmel. 'About deschooling Christianity — a response to Professor Hill' in *Journal of Christian Education* Papers 67, July 1980, pp.30–44.

Leeson, Spencer *The Public Schools Question* London, Longmans Green & Co., 1948.

Leeson, Spencer *Christian Education* London, Longmans Green & Co., 1947.

Leeson, Spencer *Christian Education Reviewed* London, Longmans Green & Co., 1957.

Lenart, Eddie. 'Advantages of a proper Christian day school' in *Elim Evangel* Vol.LXII, No.27, 11 July 1981, pp.6f.

Lester Smith, W.O *To Whom do Schools Belong?* Second edition, Oxford, Basil Blackwell, 1945.

Lester Smith, W.O.(ed.) *The School as a Christian Community* London, SCM, 1954.

Lester Smith, W.O. Review of *Christian Education in a Secular Society* (Niblett, W.R.) in *British Journal of Educational Studies* Vol.IX, No.1, November 1960, pp.79f.

Lester Smith, W.O *Government of Education* Harmondsworth, Penguin, 1965.

Lewis, C.S. 'The Humanitarian theory of punishment' chapter 14 (pp.96–114) in Hooper, Walter (ed.) *First and Second Things. Essays on Theology and Ethics* London, Collins, 1985.

Lincoln Diocese *Growing With the Church. The Diocesan Syllabus of Religious Education for use in Church Schools* Lincoln Diocesan Education Committee, 1974.

Linke, Miriam. 'Religion in education — a personal view' in *Primary Education Review* No.9, Autumn 1980, p.12.

Lister, David. 'Muslims may soon get their own school' in *Times Educational Supplement* No.3609, 30 August, 1985, p.5.

Livingstone, Richard *The Future in Education* London, Cambridge University Press, 1941.

Livingstone, Richard *Education For a World Adrift* London, Cambridge University Press, 1944.

Lodge, Bert. 'Church schools "should take pupils of all faiths" ' in *Times Educational Supplement* No. 3402, 11 September 1981, p.3.

Lodge, Bert. 'Questions of faith?' in *Times Educational Supplement* No.3402, 11 September 1981, p.14.

Lodge, Bert. 'Concern over Muslim move for schools' in *Times Educational Supplement* No.3476, 11 February 1983, p.6.

Lodge, Bert 'Muslim bid to take over five schools to be discussed with DES official' in *Times Educational Supplement* No.3477, 18 February 1983, p.5.

Lodge, Bert. 'Church of England school handover plan' in *Times Educational Supplement* No.3533, 16 March 1984, p.1.

Lodge, Bert. 'Muslims reject Swann proposals' in *Times Educational Supplement* No.3645, 9 May 1986, p.1.

Lodge, Bert. 'Anglican schools "putting children off Christianity" ' in *Times Educational Supplement* No.3660, 22 August 1986, p.9.

Lodge, Bert. 'Anglican applicants still getting first priority' in *Times Educational Supplement* No.3664, 19 September 1986, p.9.

Lodge, Bert. 'Clergy fears opting out will close its schools' in *Times Educational Supplement* No.3725, 20 November 1987, p.3.

Lodge, Bert. 'Churches find no solace' in *Times Educational Supplement* No.3726, 27 November, 1987, p.5.

Lodge, Bert. 'Rumbold argues against changing RE status' in *Times Educational Supplement* No.3732, 8 January 1988, p.6.

Longley, Clifford. 'Facing the yawning gap between our culture and religious faith' in *The Times* 7 March 1988, p.14.

Loosemore, Alan. 'RE in the curriculum' in *Methodist Recorder* 14 January 1988, p.12.

Lord, E. and Bailey, Charles (eds.) *A Reader in Religious and Moral Education* London, SCM, 1973.

Loukes, Harold *Teenage Religion* London, SCM, 1961.

Loukes, Harold *New Ground in Religious Education* London, SCM, 1965.

Lush, Michael *All Age Activities for Learning and Worship* London, Scripture Union, 1983.

Lyon, David *The Steeple's Shadow: the Myths and Realities of Secularization* London, SPCK, 1985.

MacIntyre, Alasdair *Secularization and Moral Change* London, OUP, 1967.

Macaulay, Susan Schaeffer *For the Children's Sake. Educational Foundations for Home and School* Eastbourne, Kingsway Publications, 1984.

Maclure, Stuart. 'Putting one's faith in parents' in *The Tablet* Vol.241, No.7682, 10 October 1987, Educational Supplement No.52, pp.1088f.

Madge, Violet *Children in Search of Meaning. A Study of Religious and Scientific Thought and Enquiry Arising from Experiences in the Primary School Years* London, SCM, 1965.

Manchester Diocese *Guidelines for Religious Education in Church Primary Schools* Manchester Diocesan Council for Education, 1983.

Manion, B.C. 'The future of Christian schools: a response' in *Journal of Christian Education* Papers 75, November 1982, pp.24–00.

Mann, Lindsey J. 'The need for Christian Education' in *Elim Evangel* Vol.LXVII, No.36, 6 September 1986, pp.8f.

Maritain, Jacques *Education at the Crossroads* Newhaven and London, Yale University Press, 1943.

Martin, Charles *You've Got to Start Somewhere When You Think About Education* Leicester, Inter-Varsity Press, 1979.

Martin, Charles *Have Schools Lost Their Way?* Nottingham, Grove Books, 1980.

Martin, Charles et al *Christian Aims in Education* Leicester, Universities and Colleges Christian Fellowship, 1983.

Martin, Charles. 'The case for State schools' in *Spectrum* Vol.16, No.1, Autumn 1983, pp.21–26.

Martin, Charles. 'Schools on the scales — County Schools: Faithless?' in *Christian Family* April 1987, pp.14f.

Martin, Charles. 'Christian Education: a response' in *Spectrum* Vol. 19, No.2, Summer 1987, pp.117–119.

Martin, Charles. Review of Hill, Brian *The Greening of Christian Education* (Lancer Books, 1985) in *Spectrum* Vol.19, No.2, Summer 1987, pp.180f.

Martin, Charles. Review of Hill, Brian *Choosing the Right School*

(Australian Teachers Christian Fellowship, 1987) in *Spectrum* Vol.20, No.1, Spring 1988, pp.92f.

Martin, Charles *Schools Now* Tring, Lion, 1988, revised edition 1989.

Martin, David *The Religious and the Secular* London, Routledge & Keegan Paul, 1969.

Martin, David *A General Theory of Secularization* Oxford, Basil Blackwell, 1978.

Mason, Charlotte M *Home Education* Thirteenth edition, London, Kegan Paul, Trench, Trubner & Co Ltd., 1930.

Mason, Charlotte M *An Essay Towards a Philosophy of Education* Third edition, London, J.M. Dent & Sons Ltd., 1954.

Mason, Charlotte M *Home and School Education* Sixth edition, Oxford, The Scrivener Press, 1953.

Mason, Charlotte M *Parents and Children* Seventh edition, Kegan Paul, Trench, Trubner & Co Ltd., n.d.

Mathews, H.F *Revolution in Religious Education* Oxford, Religious Education Press, 1966.

Matthews, M.G. 'A Christian Education conference' in *Christian Parent–Teacher League Newsletter* December 1980, pp.4f.

May, Philip R *Which Way to School?* Berkhamstead, Lion Publishing, 1972.

May, Philip R. 'Bring up your children: some reflections on Christian schools' in *Spectrum* Vol.7, No.1, pp.4–6.

May, Philip R. 'Religious judgments in children and adolescents: a research report' in *Learning for Living* Vol 16, No.3, Spring 1977, pp.115–122.

May, Philip R *Which Way to Teach?* Leicester, IVP, 1981.

May, Philip R *Confidence in the Classroom* Leicester, IVP, 1988.

May, Philip R. & Johnston, O. Raymond. 'Parental attitudes to religious education in state schools' in *Durham Research Review* Vol.V, No.18, April 1967, pp.127–138.

May, Philip R. & Johnston, O. Raymond *Religion in our Schools* London, Hodder & Stoughton, 1968.

May, Philip R. & Holloway, Colin *Preparing for Teaching: a Christian Perspective* London, IVP, 1972.

McCarthy, Rockne et al *Society, State and Schools — A Case For Structural and Confessional Pluralism* Michigan, William B. Eerdmans, 1981.

McClelland, V. Alan (ed) *Christian Education in a Pluralist Society* London, Routledge, 1988.

McIntyre, John *Multiculture and Multi-faith Societies: some Examinable Assumptions* Oxford, The Farmington Institute for Christian Studies, Occasional Paper No.3, n.d. Reprinted in *Occasional Papers 1976–1986* Oxford, Farmington Institute for Christian Studies, 1987, pp.17–22.

McLaughlin, T.H. 'Parental rights and the religious upbringing of children' in *Journal of Philosophy of Education* Vol.18, No.1, 1984, pp.75–83.

McLaughlin, T.H. 'Religion, upbringing and liberal values: a rejoinder to Eamonn Callan' in *Journal of Philosophy of Education* Vol.19, No.1, 1985, pp.119–127.

McPhail, P., Chapman, H. and Ungoed-Thomas, J.R *Moral Education in the Secondary School* London, Longman, 1972.

Methodist Conference *Christian Commitment in Education* Report of the Methodist Conference Commission on Education. London, Epworth Press, 1970.

Michell, Catherine *Christian Education and the Christian Nation: a Study of the Role Envisaged for Religious Education in British State Schools 1920–1965* Unpublished M.Litt. thesis, Cambridge University, 1985.

Millar, L *Christian Education in the First Four Centuries* London, The Faith Press. 1946.

Milson, Frederick W *Social Group Method and Christian Education* London, Chester House Publications, 1963.

Miranda, Evelina Orteza y. 'Some problems with the expression "Christian Education" ' in *British Journal of Religious Education* Vol.8, No.2, Spring 1986, pp.94–102.

Mitchell, B. 'What is Christian Education?' in *The Tablet* Vol.236, No.7407, 26 June 1982, Educational Supplement No.36, pp.645–648.

Mohon, W. R *Primary Curriculum* Publisher not stated, 1977.

Mohon, W. R *Train Up a Child* Stockton, Eunice Press, 1981.

Moran, Gabriel *Design for Religion Toward Ecumenical Education* London, Search Press,1971.

Morris, Henry M *Education for the Real World* California, Creation-Life Publishers Inc., 1977.

Mouque, David. 'Schools on the scales — Alternatives: "Christian" Schools' in *Christian Family* March 1987, p.20f.

Munby, D.L *The Idea of a Secular Society and its Significance for Christians* (Riddell Lectures 1962) London, OUP, 1963.

Murphy, James *Church State and Schools in Britain 1800–1970* London, Routledge and Kegan Paul, 1971.

Murray, A. Victor *Education Into Religion* London, Nisbet & Co. Ltd., 1953.

Murray, John *Collected Writings of John Murray* Edinburgh, The Banner of Truth Trust, 1976, (Vol.1 Chapter 49 'Christian Education' pp.367–374).

Murtagh, Mary *Parents Children and Faith* London, Family and Social Action, 1985.

National Society. *The Content of Agreed Syllabuses and Biblical Scholarship To-day* London, The National Society, n.d.

National Society. *Education — Christian or Secular?* London, The National Society, 1967.

National Society. *What is a Church School?* London, The National Society, 1967.

National Society. *Manual for Church Schools* London, The National Society (Church of England) for Promoting Religious Education, 1981.

National Union of Teachers. *Into the 70s A Discussion Document* London, NUT, 1969.

National Union of Teachers. *Religious Education in a Multifaith Society* London, NUT, 1984.

Neuhaus, R.J. *Democracy and the Renewal of Public Education* Michigan, William B. Eerdmans, 1987.

Newbigin, L. *Honest Religion for Secular Man* London, SCM, 1966.

Newbigin, L. 'Teaching Religion in a secular plural society' in *Learning for Living* Vol.17, No.2, Winter 1977, pp.82–88, reprinted in Hull, J.M. (ed) *New Directions in Religious Education* Basingstoke, Falmer Press, 1982.

Newsom Report *Half our Future* London, HMSO, 1963.

Newsome, David. *Godliness and Good Learning* London, John Murray, 1961.

Niblett, W.R. *Christian Education in a Secular Society* London, Oxford University Press, 1960.

Niblett, W.R. (ed.). *Moral Education in a Changing Society* London, Faber, 1963.

Niblett, Roy. Review of *Commitment and Neutrality in Religious Education* (Hulmes, E. Chapman, 1979) and of *Teaching God* (Tilby, Angela. Fount, 1979) in *Theology* Vol.LXXXIII, No.695, September 1980, pp.394–396.

Niblett, Roy. 'Christian education: authority and communication' in *British Journal of Religious Education* Vol.4, No.2, Spring 1982, pp.76–79.

Nichols, Kevin. 'Taking stock of the Catholic school' in *The Tablet* Vol.237, No.7454, 21 May 1983, Educational Supplement No.39, pp.478–480.

Nipkow, K. E. 'Theological and educational concepts — problems of integration and differentiation' in *British Journal of Religious Education* Vol.1, No.1, Autumn 1978, pp.3–13.

Northamptonshire Agreed Syllabus of Religious Education (Primary Section). 1968.

O'Connor, Maureen. 'Touching faith and the future' in *The Guardian* 26 June 1984, p.11.

O'Gorman, Kathleen. 'Catholic identity crisis' in *The Tablet* Vol.241, No.7682, 10 October 1987, Educational Supplement No.52, pp.1091–1093.

O'Keefe, Bernadette. 'Schools for all faiths' in *The Tablet* Vol.237, No.7454, 21 May 1983, Educational Supplement No.39, pp.482f.

O'Keefe, Bernadette. *Faith, Culture and the Dual System A Comparative Study of Church and County Schools* London, Falmer Press, 1986.

O'Keefe, Bernadette. 'A balance for our schools' in *Journal of Beliefs and Values* Vol.7, No.2, 1986, pp.1–13.

O'Keefe, Bernadette. Review of Francis, L. *Partnership in Rural*

Education London, Collins, 1986 in *Journal of Beliefs and Values* Vol.8, No.1, 1987, pp.26–28.

Old, Margaret V. *Seven Plus A Handbook for Teachers and Leaders Working With Sevens to Tens in the Church* London, Scripture Union, 1972.

Old, Margaret V. *Today's Children, Tomorrow's Church* London, Scripture Union, 1974.

Oldham, J.H. *The Churches Survey Their Task* The report of the conference at Oxford, July 1937, on church, community and State. London, George Allen & Unwin Ltd., 1937.

Order of Christian Unity. *Ways Whereby Christian Education in State Schools Should be Saved* Second edition, London, OCU, 1976.

Order of Christian Unity. *Curriculum Christianity* London, Unity Press, 1977.

Otter, J.L. *Nathaniel Woodard: a Memoir of His Life* London, Lane, 1925.

Owen, Roger. 'Schools on the scales — Accelerated Christian Education' in *Family* April 1985, pp.9–13.

Owen, Roger. 'Schools on the scales — governors: parent power' in *Christian Family* March 1987, pp.20f.

Packer, J.I. *Keep Yourselves From Idols A Discussion of the Book Honest to God* London, Church Book Room Press, 1963.

Pannikkar, Raimundo. *Worship and Secular Man* London, Darton Longman & Todd, 1973.

Partnership in Christian Education London, The Institute of Christian Education, 1962.

Patterson, R.G. 'The alternative Christian school: a response' in *Journal of Christian Education* Papers 75, November 1982, pp.31–37.

Person, Peter P. *An Introduction to Christian Education* Grand Rapids, Michigan, Baker Book House, 1958.

Peters, R.S. 'Reason and habit: the paradox of moral education' in Niblett, W.R. (ed.) *Moral Education in a Changing Society* London, Faber, 1963.

Peters, R.S. *Ethics and Education* London, George Allen & Unwin, 1966.

Peterson, Michael L. *Philosophy of Education: Issues and Options* (Contours of Christian Philosophy series) Leicester, IVP, 1986.

Pointer, Roy. 'Church growth in England?' in *Prospects for the Eighties* Vol.2, London, Marc Europe, 1983.

Poole, Michael W. *Watch the Language* (No.1 in The Bloxham Project 'Models in science and religion' series). Bloxham Project, 1984.

Poole, Michael, W. ''. . . And May be Used in Evidence''* (No.3 in The Bloxham Project 'Models in science and religion' series). Bloxham Project, 1984.

Poole, Michael, W. *Some Uses and Abuses of Models* (No.6 in The

Bloxham Project 'Models in science and religion' series). Bloxham Project, 1984.

Pott, David. 'Teaching in three contexts — a study in contrasts' in *Spectrum* Vol.16, No.1, Autumn 1983, pp.15–17.

Pratt, Vernon. *Religion and Secularisation* London, Macmillan, 1970.

Priestley, J. 'Teaching transcendence' in *Aspects of Education* No.28, 1982, pp.5–21.

Rahner, Karl (ed.). *Sacramentum Mundi: An Encyclopedia of Theology* London, Burns and Oates, Vol.3, 1969.

Ramsey, I.T. 'Discernment, commitment, and cosmic disclosure' in *Religious Education* Vol.LX, September 1965, pp.10–14.

Ramsey, I.T. 'Towards a theology of education' in *Learning for Living* Vol.15, No.4, Summer 1976, pp.137–147.

Ree, H.A. *The Essential Grammar School* London, George Harrap, 1956.

Reid, Mike. See Smith, Peter.

Reid, Mary. 'Separation or segregation' in *Family* April 1985, pp.11–13.

Religious Education in a Diverse Society — A Discussion Paper Prepared by a Working Party for the attention of the Catholic Association for Racial Justice and the Committee for Community Relations of the Catholic Bishops' Conference of England and Wales. London, Catholic Association for Racial Justice and Committee for Community Relations, 1987.

Richards, Lawrence O. *A Theology of Christian Education* Grand Rapids, Michigan, Zondervan Publishing House, 1975.

Richards, Norman A. *The Determinants of Pluralism in Religious Education* Unpublished M.Ed. thesis, University of Durham, 1980.

Richards, Norman A. 'Is there a prophet in the house?' in *Spectrum* Vol.18, No.1, Spring 1986, pp.17–23.

Richardson, Robin & Chapman, John. *Images of Life Problems of Religious Belief and Human Relations in Schools* (Bloxham Project Research Unit) London, SCM, 1973.

Robinson, E. *The Original Vision* Oxford, Religious Experience Research Unit, 1977.

Robinson, E. *The Language of Mystery* London, SCM, 1987.

Robinson, John A.T. *Honest to God* London, SCM, 1963.

Robinson, John A.T. & Edwards, David L. *The Honest to God Debate* London, SCM, 1963.

Robinson, John A.T. *But That I Can't Believe* London, Collins, 1967.

Robinson, Wheeler H. *The Christian Doctrine of Man* Edinburgh, T. & T. Clark, 1911.

Robson, G.W. 'Christian Education is meaningful: a reply' (to the immediately preceding article by Hirst, P.H.) in *Faith and Thought* Vol.99, No.1, October 1971, pp.55–60.

Rochester Diocese. *The Rochester Statement. Papers on the Church and Education* The Rochester Diocesan Board of Education, 1985.

Rodgers, John. *The Old Public Schools of England* London, B.T. Batsford Ltd., 1938.

Rogers, Rick. 'Denominational schooling' in *NAME Journal* Vol.10, No.1, Autumn 1981, pp.26–33.

Rogers, Rick. 'Separated brethren' in *The Guardian* 8 December 1981, p.11.

Rogers, Rick. 'Church schools — time to look again' in *Where* No.179, June 1982, pp.6–13.

Rossiter, Graham M. *An Interpretation of Normative Theory for Religious Education in Australian Schools* Unpublished PhD thesis, Macquarie University, 1983 (copy in Birmingham University Faculty of Education library).

Rudman, Stanley. Review of Hull, J.M. *What Prevents Christian Adults From Learning?* (SCM, 1985) in *Modern Theology* Vol.3, No.4, July 1987, pp.376–378.

Runcie, Robert. 'Christian Education' in *Windows Onto God* London, SPCK, 1983, pp.74–85.

Russell, Conrad. 'A time to reform' in *Times Educational Supplement* No.3360, 14 November 1980, p.4.

Russell, Eric. *I Want to Teach RE* London, Church Pastoral Aid Society, 1974.

Sacks, Benjamin. *The Religious Issue in the State Schools of England and Wales 1902–1914 a Nation's Quest for Human Dignity* New Mexico, The University of New Mexico Press, 1961.

St John-Stevas, Norman. 'Religious and moral values in schools' in *The Tablet* 18 February 1984, Educational Supplement No.41, pp.160–162.

St. Mary's Centre. *Church Schools in Berkshire — Their Place and Relevance in the 1980s* St.Mary's Centre Paper No.4., n.d.

Sallnow, Theresa. 'Truly Catholic schools' in *The Tablet* 8 October 1983, Educational Supplement No.40, pp.977–979.

Sandhurst, B.G. *How Heathen is Britain?* London, Collins, 1946.

Sankey, D. *Science, Religion and the School Curriculum* Discussion Paper No.2, Oxford, The Farmington Institute for Christian Studies, n.d.

Saunders, Betty. 'New Education Bill comes under fire from Church Board' in *Church Times* No.6503, 2 October 1987, pp.1 & 24.

Schaeffer Macaulay, Susan. See Macaulay, Susan Schaeffer.

Schools Council *The Humanities Project: An Introduction* London, Heinemann Educational, 1970.

Schools Council *Religious Education in Secondary Schools* (Schools Council Working Paper 36) London, Evans/Methuen Educational, 1971.

Schools Council *The Whole Curriculum* (Schools Council Working Paper 53) London, Evans/Methuen Educational, 1975.

Scotland, Nigel. 'Why should religion be studied in schools?' (Part 1) in *Religious Studies Today* Vol.10, No.2, Spring 1985, pp.7–14.

Scotland, Nigel. 'Why should religion be studied in schools?' (Part 2) in *Religious Studies Today* Vol.10, No.3, Summer 1985, pp.3–6.

Scotland, Nigel. *The Changing Face of R.E.* Leicester, UCCF, 1986.

Secondary Education For All: a New Drive (Government White Paper) Cmnd.604, London, HMSO, 1958.

Secondary Examinations Council, Working Paper 1 *Differentiated Assessment in GCSE* London, SEC, 1985.

Seton, Marie. 'A system worth saving' in *The Tablet* Vol.242, No.7701, 20 February 1988, Educational Supplement No.53, pp.206f.

Sharp, Brian J. *Partners in Learning* Teaching material for the five and six year old based on the BLC Syllabus *Experience and Faith.* London, Methodist Youth Department and Nutfield, National Christian Education Council, 1972.

Sheffield Diocese. *A Handbook of Suggestions for Church Schools* Diocese of Sheffield, 1985.

Sherman, Jill. 'Shut down church schools says bishop' in *Times Educational Supplement* No.3656, 25 July 1986, p.1.

Sherrington, Edwina. *Christian Ministry and Further Education. The report on a project 1982–5* Publisher not stated. Published 1985.

Short, Edward. *Education in a Changing World* London, Pitman Publishing, 1971.

Sidey, Ken. 'Christ in the Classroom' in *Moody Monthly* March 1986, pp.26–29.

Silver, Pamela & Harold. *The Education of the Poor — the History of a National School 1824–1974* London, Routledge & Kegan Paul, 1974.

Simonds, Robert L. *Communicating a Christian World View in the Classroom* California, National Association of Christian Educators, 1983.

Smart, N. *The Teacher and Christian Belief* London, James Clarke Co. Ltd., 1966.

Smart, N. *Secular Education and the Logic of Religion* London, Faber and Faber Ltd., 1968.

Smart, N. & Horder, D. *New Movements in Religious Education* London, Temple Smith, 1975.

Smith, J.W.D. *Religious Education in a Secular Setting* London, SCM, 1969.

Smith, J.W.D. 'How Christian can State schools be today?' in *Learning for Living* Vol.9. No.4 March 1970 pp.7–9.

Smith, Michael B. 'An open invitation to visit Emmanuel Christian School' in *Elim Evangel* Vol.LXII, No.28, 18 July 1981, p.5.

Smith, Peter. 'Christian Education' editorial in *Elim Evangel* Vol.LXVII, No.36, 6 September 1986, p.2.

Smith, Peter. 'Face to face with Pastor Mike Reid' (Principal of Peniel Academy, Brentwood) in *Elim Evangel* Vol.LXVIII, No.44, 31 October 1987, pp.4f.

Smith, W.O. Lester. See Lester Smith, W.O.

Smoker, Barbara. *What's This Humanism?* London, BHA, n.d.

Social Morality Council. *Moral and Religious Education in County Schools* London, Social Morality Council, 1970.

Social Trends 17 London, HMSO, 1987.

Social Trends 18 London, HMSO, 1988.

Souper, Patrick C.and Kay, William K. *The School Assembly in Hampshire* Southampton, University of Southampton, 1982.

Souper, Patrick C. and Kay, William K. *The School Assembly Debate: 1942–1982* Southampton, University of Southampton, 1983.

Souper, Patrick C. and Kay, William K. *Worship in the Independent Day School* Southampton, University of Southampton, 1983.

Southwark Diocese. *The Ethos of a Church School* Working Party for Multi-ethnic Education Working Paper No.1 London, Southwark Diocesan Board of Education, 1983.

Stanford, E.C.D. *Education in Focus, the Pattern of the School Community* Wallington, The Religious Education Press Ltd., 1965.

Stanton, Mary. *Education: a System With Design* Florida, Ambassadors International, 1976.

Statistics of Education 1979: Schools Vol.1 London, HMSO, 1981.

Steensma, Geraldine J. & Van Brummelen, Harro W. *Shaping School Curriculum: a Biblical View* Indiana, Signal Publishing, 1977.

Stenhouse, L. 'The Humanities Curriculum Project' in *Journal of Curriculum Studies* Vol.1, No. 1, November 1968, pp.26–33.

Storkey, Alan. *A Christian Social Perspective* Leicester, IVP, 1979.

Storkey, Alan. 'The case for Christian schools' in *Spectrum* Vol.16, No.1, Autumn 1983, pp. 4–14.

Strawson, William. *Teachers and the New Theology* London, Epworth Press, 1969.

Strudwick, V., Meyer, C., and Gay, J. *The Debate About Church Schools in the Oxford Diocese* Oxford diocese n.d.

Sutcliffe, Jeremy. 'Evangelical schools seek to opt in' in *Times Educational Supplement* No.3733, 15 January 1988, p.7.

Sutcliffe, John M. *Learning and Teaching Together* London, Chester House Publications, 1980.

Sutcliffe, John M. 'Christian teachers in county schools' *Association of Religious Education Bulletin* No.36, Vol.14, 1981, pp.10–15.

Swann Report *Education for all* (The Report of the Committee of Inquiry into the Education of Children from Ethnic Minority Groups) Cmnd. 9453, London, HMSO, 1985.

Tait, Eddie. 'The Christian alternatives to state education' in *Revival* September/October 1981, pp.10f.

Tarasar, Constance J. (ed.) *Perspectives on Orthodox Education* Report of the International Orthodox Education Consultation for Rural/Developing Areas. New York, Syndesmos and The Department of Religious Education of the Orthodox Church in America, 1983.

Taylor, G. & Saunders, J.B. *The Law of Education* Eighth edition, London, Butterworth, 1976.

Taylor, Paul. 'Opt In, Not Out' in *Evangelicals Now* Vol.II, No.12, December 1987, p.17.

Technical Education Cmd. 9703, London, HMSO, 1956.

Thatcher, Adrian. 'The recovery of Christian education' in *Scottish Journal of Theology* Vol.40, No.3, 1987, pp.437–450.

Third Way/Shaftesbury Project. *Education — Schooling for the Future* New Malden, Third Way & Nottingham, The Shaftesbury Project, n.d.

Tidball, Derek. *A World Without Windows: Living as a Christian in a Secular World* London, Scripture Union, 1987.

Tilby, Angela. *Teaching God* London, Collins, 1979.

Times Educational Supplement No.3706, 10 July 1987, 'Church leaders warn against breaking away' p.1.

Tirrell, Leslie B. *The Aided Schools Handbook* Second edition. London, National Society and SPCK, 1969.

Todd, Noel. 'Church schools' in *Religious Studies Today* Vol.1, No.2, Spring 1976, pp2f.

Todd, Noel. 'Christian Education for all?' in *ACT Now* No.3, Summer 1984, pp.12f.

Todd, Noel. 'The Church of England school: in pursuit of a Christian tradition' in *Aspects of Education* No.35, 1986, pp.73–88.

Tonkin, Paul. 'Are we really a Christian nation?' in *Times Educational Supplement* No.3676, 12 December 1986. p.34.

Travis, Patricia M. 'State education: come out or stay in?' in *Renewal* No.106, August/September 1983, pp.20–22.

Treasure, Geoff. *What Me Sir?* London, Inter-Varsity Press, 1972.

Tulloch, Frances (ed.) *Curriculum Christianity: Crisis in the Classroom* London, Unity Press, 1977.

United Nations. *Universal Declaration of Human Rights* General Assembly of the United Nations, 1948.

Van Buren, Paul. 'Christian Education post mortem Dei' in *Religious Education* Vol.LX, January 1965, pp.4–10.

Van Til, Cornelius. *The Dilemma of Education* Second edition, Phillipsburg, Presbyterian and Reformed, 1956.

Van Til, Cornelius. *Essays on Christian Education* Phillipsburg, Presbyterian and Reformed, 1974.

Vriend, John et al. *To Prod The Slumbering Giant: Crisis, Commitment and Christian Education* Toronto, Wedge Publishing Foundation, 1972.

Wainwright, J.A. *School and Church: Partners in Christian Education* London, Oxford University Press, 1963.

Wallace, Wendy. 'God's own office work' in *Times Educational Supplement* No.3738, 19 February 1988, p.25.

Warren, C. Peter. *Comprehensive Education* Exeter, Paternoster Press, 1979.

Watson, Brenda. *Openness and Commitment* Occasional Paper No.20, Oxford, Farmington Institute, 1986.

Watson, Brenda. *Education and Belief* Blackwell, 1987.

Weeks, Noel. 'In defence of Christian schools' *Journal of Christian Education* Papers 67, July 1980, pp.21–29.

Wenham, Gordon. 'What aspects of Christian belief should be taught in county schools?' in *RE News and Views* Vol.4, No.1, Autumn 1986, pp.16f.

Westerhoff, John H. *Will Our Children Have Faith?* Minneapolis, The Winston Seabury Press, 1976.

Wigram, D.R. 'Problems of Christian schools' in *Spectrum* Vol.2, No.2, January 1970, pp.55f.

Wilkes, Keith. 'Church and state can never mix' in *Times Educational Supplement* No.3684, 6 February 1987, p.23.

Wilkins, R. *Why Educate?* Cardiff, Association of Christian Teachers of Wales, 1985.

Williams, Tricia. *Christians in School?* London, Scripture Union, 1985.

Wilson, Bryan. *Religion in Secular Society* London, Watts, 1966.

Wilson, J., Williams, N., Sugarman, B. *Introduction to Moral Education* Harmondsworth, Penguin Books, 1967.

Wolterstorff, Nicholas. *Educating for Responsible Action* Grand Rapids, Christian Schools International and Wm. B. Eerdmans, 1980.

Woman's Own.'Whatever's happened to God? You tell us!' in *Woman's Own* 26 September 1987, pp.20f.

Woodard Corporation. *The Woodard Corporation: Aims and Ideals* Ellesmere, The Woodard Corporation, 1985.

Woodward, Peter. Review of *The Bible: a child's playground* (Gobbel, Roger and Gertrude. London, SCM Press, 1986) in *Times Educational Supplement* No.3676, 12 December 1986, p.35.

Wright, D.S. *A Study of Religious Beliefs in Sixth Form Boys* University of Leeds Institute of Education, 1962.

Wynnejones, Pat. *Children Under Pressure: Growing up in a Changing World* London, Triangle/SPCK, 1987.

Wynnejones, Pat. Review of Macaulay, Susan Schaeffer. *For the Children's Sake* (Kingsway, 1986) in *Spectrum* Vol.20, No.1, Spring 1988, pp.90–92.

Yates, Joanna (ed.) *Faith for the Future. Essays on the Church in Education to Mark 175 Years of The National Society* London, The National Society and Church House Publishing, 1986.